THE MEDITERRANEAN LIFESTYLE

Fresh Flavors for a Longer Life

By

ROSINA CALABRESI

THE MEDITERRANEAN LIFESTYLE

Copyright Notice

© 2024 by Rosina Calabresi. All rights reserved.
No part of this publication may be reproduced, stored in a retrieval system, or transmitted in any form or by any means, electronic, mechanical, photocopying, recording, or otherwise, without prior written permission from the author, except as permitted by U.S. copyright law.

Disclaimer:

The information provided in this book is for educational and informational purposes only. The author and publisher are not responsible for any adverse effects or consequences resulting from the use of any suggestions or information contained in this book. The content is not intended as medical, nutritional, or professional advice, and readers should consult with a licensed healthcare provider before making any dietary or lifestyle changes.

The recipes in this book are intended to promote healthy living, but individual results may vary based on personal health conditions and preferences. By using this book, you agree to accept full responsibility for your actions and dietary choices.

THE MEDITERRANEAN LIFESTYLE

Table of Contents

Introduction

- **My Mediterranean Story**: A Personal Journey Through the Flavors of the Mediterranean
- **The Health Benefits of Mediterranean Eating**: Why Embracing the Mediterranean Lifestyle Will Transform Your Health
- **How This Book Will Guide You**: Simplifying the Mediterranean Diet and Helping You Embrace It with Ease

---

Chapter 1: The Mediterranean Diet – A Taste of Tradition

- **What Makes the Mediterranean Diet Unique?** Understanding the Foundations of Mediterranean Eating
- **Core Principles of Mediterranean Cuisine**: Fresh, Flavorful, and Full of Life
- **Essential Mediterranean Ingredients**: The Staples You'll Find in Every Mediterranean Kitchen
- **The Secret to Mediterranean Health**: Why the Mediterranean Diet Works

Chapter 2: Regional Flavors and Dishes Across the Mediterranean

- **Exploring the Rich Diversity of Mediterranean Cuisines**
- **The Tastes of Greece**: From Souvlaki to Moussaka
- **Spain's Best-Kept Secrets**: Paella, Gazpacho, and Beyond
- **Italy's Culinary Legacy**: The Eternal Influence of Olive Oil, Pasta, and Pizza
- **North African Influences**: Moroccan Tagine, Tunisian Couscous, and More

Chapter 3: Key Mediterranean Ingredients and How to Use Them

- **Olive Oil, Herbs, and Spices**: The Foundations of Mediterranean Flavor
- **The Mediterranean Pantry**: Must-Have Ingredients for Every Kitchen
- **Fresh Produce and Seafood**: Seasonal and Local Ingredients that Define the Region

Chapter 4: Mediterranean Cooking Techniques

- **Slow-Cooked Delights**: Stews, Roasts, and Braises
- **Grilling and Barbecuing**: The Mediterranean Love for Charred Flavor
- **Simple, Elegant Sauces**: Dressings, Dips, and Drizzles

Chapter 5: Breakfasts and Brunches

- **Mediterranean Morning Delights**: Frittatas, Yogurts, and Pastries

THE MEDITERRANEAN LIFESTYLE

- **Fresh and Hearty Starts to Your Day**: Mediterranean-Inspired Smoothies, Toasts, and More

Chapter 6: Appetizers and Small Plates

- **Meze and Tapas**: Mediterranean Snacks to Share
- **Classic Dips**: Hummus, Tzatziki, and Baba Ghanoush
- **Stuffed Delights**: Grape Leaves, Pastries, and Pockets

Chapter 7: Salads and Sides

- **Mediterranean Salads**: Fresh, Vibrant, and Healthy
- **Roasted Vegetables and Grains**: Simple Sides to Complement Any Meal
- **Breads and Flatbreads**: Pita, Focaccia, and Beyond

Chapter 8: Soups and Stews

- **Hearty Mediterranean Soups**: From Greek Avgolemono to Spanish Sopa de Ajo
- **Slow-Cooked Stews**: Moroccan Lamb, Tunisian Harira, and More

Chapter 9: Seafood and Fish

- **Mediterranean Sea Bounty**: Grilled Fish, Seafood Paella, and More
- **Healthy, Flavorful, and Fresh**: Mediterranean Fish Dishes You'll Love

Chapter 10: Poultry and Meat

- **Chicken, Lamb, and Goat**: The Meats of Mediterranean Cuisine
- **Classic Meat Dishes**: From Greek Lamb to Spanish Cochineal

Chapter 11: Pasta and Grains

- **Italian Pasta Perfection**: Sauces, Shapes, and Simple Dishes
- **Grain-Based Delights**: Couscous, Risotto, and Beyond

Chapter 12: Vegetarian and Vegan Mediterranean Dishes

- **Plant-Based Mediterranean**: Flavors that Shine without Meat
- **Healthy, Vibrant Dishes**: From Veggie-Loaded Tagine to Stuffed Eggplant

Chapter 13: Mediterranean Desserts

- **Sweet Mediterranean Treats**: Baklava, Tiramisu, and More
- **Fruit-Based Delights**: Sorbets, Cakes, and Pies

Chapter 14: Drinks and Beverages

- **Mediterranean Wines and Spirits**: Pairing the Best Wines with Mediterranean Flavors
- **Refreshing Drinks**: Lemonades, Herbal Teas, and Coffee

Chapter 15: Entertaining Mediterranean Style

- **Mediterranean Feasts**: How to Host a Perfect Dinner Party
- **Creating the Right Atmosphere**: Table Settings and Atmosphere

Chapter 16: The Mediterranean Diet in Everyday Life

- **Meal Planning for the Mediterranean Diet**: Simple Steps for Success
- **Cooking for One, Two, or a Family**: Adapting Mediterranean Meals for Every Need

Chapter 17: The Health Benefits of Mediterranean Eating

- **Improved Heart Health**: How the Mediterranean Diet Promotes a Strong Heart
- **Weight Loss and Management**: The Role of Mediterranean Eating in Maintaining a Healthy Weight
- **Mental and Emotional Wellness**: How Mediterranean Eating Can Improve Your Mood and Mind

Chapter 18: Shopping and Sourcing Mediterranean Ingredients

- **Where to Find Fresh Mediterranean Ingredients**: Farmers' Markets, Specialty Stores, and Online Sources
- **Choosing Quality Products**: Olive Oil, Cheese, and More

Chapter 19: Mediterranean Lifestyle Beyond the Plate

- **Active Living**: Mediterranean Fitness and Outdoor Activities
- **The Mediterranean Approach to Socializing**: Dining, Family, and Community

Chapter 20: Adapting the Mediterranean Diet to Your Own Taste

- **Personalizing Mediterranean Dishes**: Adjusting Recipes to Fit Your Preferences
- **Creating Your Own Mediterranean Recipes**: How to Experiment and Explore

---

Appendices

- **Conversion Tables**: Metric vs. Imperial Measurements
- **Index of Mediterranean Ingredients and Recipes**
- **Glossary of Mediterranean Cooking Terms**

THE MEDITERRANEAN LIFESTYLE

Introduction

My Mediterranean Story: A Personal Journey Through the Flavors of the Mediterranean

As a passionate lover of food, I have always been captivated by the rich, vibrant flavors of the Mediterranean. My first encounter with Mediterranean cuisine was not through a cookbook or a trendy restaurant but on a journey through the Mediterranean itself—savoring the simple yet exquisite dishes served on sun-drenched terraces, feeling the warm breeze of the sea, and learning the stories behind each meal. From the olive orchards of Greece to the coastal markets of Italy, I discovered that Mediterranean cooking is much more than just a style of food; it's a way of life.

Each meal I experienced had its own story, deeply rooted in tradition, history, and a connection to the land and sea. In Italy, I learned that pasta wasn't just a dish but an expression of family and culture. In Morocco, I discovered the art of slow-cooked tagine and the use of spices that transform a dish into an aromatic adventure. In Greece, I tasted the purity of olive oil and fresh vegetables, honoring the natural bounty of the land. The food I tasted was always fresh, healthy, and rooted in the seasons, which is what first drew me to the Mediterranean way of eating.

This book is not just a collection of recipes—it is an invitation to embark on your own Mediterranean journey. Through each page, you will discover how to incorporate these flavors into your own kitchen, bringing the heart of the Mediterranean into your everyday life. I hope that by sharing my personal experience, you will not only appreciate the joy of Mediterranean food but also experience its transformative power in your own health and wellbeing.

The Health Benefits of Mediterranean Eating: Why Embracing the Mediterranean Lifestyle Will Transform Your Health

The Mediterranean diet is often hailed as one of the healthiest in the world—and for good reason. It is more than just a way of eating; it's a lifestyle that has been proven to reduce the risk of chronic diseases, promote heart health, and enhance longevity. This diet has been studied extensively, and research consistently supports its benefits.

One of the most striking aspects of Mediterranean eating is its emphasis on whole, minimally processed foods. By incorporating fresh fruits, vegetables, whole grains, legumes, nuts, and healthy fats like olive oil into your meals, you nourish your body with the nutrients it needs to thrive. This diet is naturally anti-inflammatory, supporting better immune function and reducing the risk of conditions like heart disease, type 2 diabetes, and certain cancers.

But it's not just about the food—it's also about how you eat. The Mediterranean lifestyle encourages meals to be enjoyed with family and friends, in a relaxed and unhurried atmosphere. This practice of mindful eating promotes better digestion, satisfaction, and a deeper connection to food. By embracing this approach, many people experience a reduction in stress, improved mental health, and a more balanced lifestyle overall.

Perhaps the most compelling evidence for the Mediterranean diet's transformative effects lies in its long-term benefits. Studies have shown that those who follow a Mediterranean diet live longer, healthier lives, with a reduced risk of cognitive decline, obesity, and metabolic syndrome. It's a diet that isn't just about looking good today—it's about feeling great for years to come.

How This Book Will Guide You: Simplifying the Mediterranean Diet and Helping You Embrace It with Ease

This book was created with one clear mission in mind: to make the Mediterranean diet accessible and enjoyable for everyone. Whether you are a seasoned cook or a complete beginner, this guide will simplify the process of incorporating Mediterranean principles into your daily routine.

You might be wondering, "Where do I start?" The beauty of Mediterranean cuisine is that it doesn't require complicated techniques or hard-to-find ingredients. The focus is on simplicity, quality, and balance. In the following chapters, I will introduce you to the core principles of Mediterranean eating, break down essential ingredients, and guide you through easy-to-follow recipes that anyone can make at home.

Each recipe is designed to be straightforward and practical, with an emphasis on fresh, seasonal ingredients that you can easily find in your local grocery store or farmer's market. I will also share tips on how to make the most out of your ingredients, how to balance your meals for maximum health benefits, and how to approach cooking with the relaxed, joyful attitude that defines Mediterranean culture.

You don't need to overhaul your entire lifestyle overnight. With this book, I'll help you gradually integrate Mediterranean flavors and principles into your life in a way that's sustainable and enjoyable. By the end of this book, you'll have the tools, knowledge, and confidence to embrace the Mediterranean way of eating—and transform your health in the process.

THE MEDITERRANEAN LIFESTYLE

Closing Thoughts for the Introduction:

The Mediterranean diet is about more than just food—it's a philosophy that has been passed down through generations, a way of honoring the land, the seasons, and the people we share our meals with. Whether you're looking to improve your health, discover new flavors, or simply enjoy meals with your loved ones, the Mediterranean lifestyle offers something for everyone.

So, let's begin this journey together. With each chapter, recipe, and tip, you'll be taking small steps toward a healthier, more fulfilling way of living—one that is rooted in the heart of the Mediterranean.

Chapter 1:

The Mediterranean Diet – A Taste of Tradition

What Makes the Mediterranean Diet Unique?

Understanding the Foundations of Mediterranean Eating

The Mediterranean diet stands apart from other dietary approaches for its seamless blend of health, flavor, and cultural significance. It's not just a diet—it's a way of life that has been cultivated over centuries by the countries bordering the Mediterranean Sea, including Greece, Italy, Spain, Turkey, and Morocco, among others.

The uniqueness of the Mediterranean diet lies in its emphasis on simplicity, seasonality, and quality over quantity. Unlike restrictive diets that eliminate entire food groups or rely heavily on processed "diet" foods, the Mediterranean diet celebrates wholesome, natural ingredients. It is an inclusive, flexible approach to eating, making it sustainable and enjoyable for people from all walks of life.

Key Features That Set the Mediterranean Diet Apart

1. **Fresh, Seasonal Ingredients**:
   At its core, the Mediterranean diet is rooted in the use of fresh, locally sourced ingredients. Seasonal produce such as tomatoes, eggplants, peppers, citrus fruits, and leafy greens take center stage in Mediterranean dishes, ensuring that meals are bursting with flavor and nutrition.
2. **Healthy Fats as the Foundation**:
   Olive oil, often referred to as "liquid gold," is the cornerstone of Mediterranean cooking. It's rich in monounsaturated fats, antioxidants, and anti-inflammatory properties, making it a healthy and flavorful alternative to butter or margarine. Other sources of healthy fats, such as nuts, seeds, and avocados, further enrich the diet.
3. **A Plant-Forward Approach**:
   While the Mediterranean diet includes animal proteins like fish, chicken, and dairy, it prioritizes plant-based foods. Meals are built around vegetables, legumes, grains, and

fruits, with meat and fish serving as complements rather than the centerpiece. This balance promotes overall health and reduces environmental impact.

4. **Seafood as a Staple**:
   The proximity to the Mediterranean Sea has influenced the heavy reliance on seafood in this diet. Fish like sardines, mackerel, and salmon are rich in omega-3 fatty acids, essential for heart and brain health.

5. **Whole Grains and Legumes**:
   Refined grains are rarely found in traditional Mediterranean cooking. Instead, whole grains like farro, bulgur, couscous, and barley are staples, providing sustained energy and dietary fiber. Legumes such as chickpeas, lentils, and beans are also integral, adding protein and texture to dishes.

6. **Herbs and Spices Over Salt**:
   Flavor in the Mediterranean diet comes from an array of herbs and spices, such as basil, oregano, rosemary, thyme, and saffron. These not only enhance the taste of dishes but also add health benefits due to their antioxidant and anti-inflammatory properties.

7. **Moderate and Mindful Eating**:
   Portion sizes in Mediterranean meals are typically moderate, and meals are eaten slowly and mindfully. This promotes better digestion and allows individuals to enjoy their food fully. Wine is consumed in moderation, often alongside meals, emphasizing quality over quantity.

8. **Community and Connection**:
   Food in Mediterranean cultures is deeply intertwined with family and community. Meals are social occasions, enjoyed with loved ones and accompanied by lively conversations. This emphasis on connection reduces stress and fosters a positive relationship with food.

Why the Mediterranean Diet Stands the Test of Time

The Mediterranean diet is not a new fad—it's a timeless way of eating that has evolved naturally over generations. The people of the Mediterranean have long understood the importance of eating with the seasons, using what is locally available, and preserving the integrity of food through simple preparation methods.

This diet has gained worldwide recognition because it is both sustainable and practical. It does not require specialized products, expensive ingredients, or elaborate cooking techniques. Instead, it encourages home cooking with easily accessible ingredients, making it adaptable to modern lifestyles.

THE MEDITERRANEAN LIFESTYLE

Moreover, the Mediterranean diet has been extensively studied and endorsed by health organizations around the globe. Its benefits extend beyond physical health to mental and emotional well-being, offering a holistic approach to living a healthier, happier life.

Core Principles of Mediterranean Cuisine: Fresh, Flavorful, and Full of Life

The Mediterranean diet isn't just a series of recipes; it's a philosophy rooted in tradition and a celebration of the land and sea. The core principles of Mediterranean cuisine are embracing fresh, wholesome ingredients and creating vibrant, satisfying meals that nourish both the body and soul.

1. **Simplicity and Seasonal Freshness**:
   Mediterranean cooking is centered on simplicity. Dishes are often composed of just a few ingredients, but each is chosen for its quality and natural flavor. The beauty of Mediterranean food lies in its ability to transform humble ingredients into something extraordinary. Whether it's a vine-ripened tomato drizzled with olive oil or a handful of fresh basil scattered over a pasta dish, the flavors are always vibrant and alive, reflecting the seasons.
2. **Balance**:
   The Mediterranean way of eating is based on balance, with an emphasis on moderation. Meals typically contain a healthy balance of carbohydrates, fats, and proteins, with a focus on plant-based foods. Meat is eaten in smaller quantities, and fish and legumes become the primary sources of protein. This balanced approach ensures that meals are both satisfying and heart-healthy.
3. **Celebration of Shared Meals**:
   Another defining characteristic of Mediterranean cuisine is the importance of shared meals. Food is meant to be enjoyed in the company of others—whether it's a family gathering, a casual meal with friends, or a holiday feast. The act of sharing food strengthens bonds and nurtures a sense of community, making every meal an occasion.

Essential Mediterranean Ingredients: The Staples You'll Find in Every Mediterranean Kitchen

To truly embrace the Mediterranean way of eating, it's essential to stock your kitchen with a few key ingredients that form the foundation of most dishes. These ingredients are not only flavorful but also nutritious, contributing to the health benefits of the Mediterranean diet.

THE MEDITERRANEAN LIFESTYLE

1. **Extra Virgin Olive Oil**:
   Olive oil is the heart and soul of Mediterranean cooking. Used for everything from dressing salads to sautéing vegetables, extra virgin olive oil provides a rich, fruity flavor and is packed with heart-healthy monounsaturated fats. It's also a powerful antioxidant, making it one of the healthiest oils to use in cooking.

2. **Fresh Vegetables**:
   Vegetables are the backbone of Mediterranean meals. Tomatoes, cucumbers, eggplants, peppers, spinach, and zucchini are staples in Mediterranean kitchens. These vegetables not only add color and texture to dishes but also provide an abundance of vitamins, minerals, and fiber that promote overall health.

3. **Legumes and Beans**:
   Beans, lentils, and chickpeas are essential to Mediterranean diets. They're an excellent source of plant-based protein and fiber, making them ideal for maintaining stable blood sugar levels and improving digestive health. Legumes are often used in salads, stews, and soups, adding both richness and substance to meals.

4. **Whole Grains**:
   Unlike refined grains, whole grains like bulgur, quinoa, farro, and barley are staples in Mediterranean cuisine. These grains are rich in fiber, which aids digestion, and are often used as the base for salads, pilafs, and side dishes. Whole grains also help sustain energy levels, keeping you feeling fuller for longer.

5. **Herbs and Spices**:
   Mediterranean food is all about enhancing natural flavors, and this is where herbs and spices come in. Fresh herbs like basil, oregano, thyme, mint, and rosemary are frequently used, along with spices such as cumin, saffron, paprika, and garlic. These herbs and spices not only add incredible flavor but also offer various health benefits, including anti-inflammatory and antioxidant properties.

6. **Fish and Seafood**:
   As the Mediterranean diet is built on a foundation of access to the sea, fish and seafood play a central role. Rich in omega-3 fatty acids, fishlike salmon, sardines, and mackerel are celebrated for their heart-healthy benefits. Shellfish, octopus, and squid are also commonly used, adding variety and texture to Mediterranean dishes.

The Secret to Mediterranean Health: Why the Mediterranean Diet Works

The Mediterranean diet is often praised for its numerous health benefits. It's been linked to a lower risk of chronic diseases, such as heart disease, diabetes, and even some cancers. But what is it about this way of eating that makes it so effective?

THE MEDITERRANEAN LIFESTYLE

1. **Heart Health**:
   One of the most significant benefits of the Mediterranean diet is its impact on heart health. The diet is rich in monounsaturated fats from olive oil and omega-3 fatty acids from fish, both of which are known to reduce bad cholesterol levels and lower the risk of cardiovascular diseases. Studies have shown that the Mediterranean diet can help reduce the risk of heart attacks and strokes by up to 30%.

2. **Weight Management**:
   While the Mediterranean diet isn't a "weight loss" plan per se, it promotes healthy, sustainable weight management. The emphasis on fiber-rich vegetables, legumes, and whole grains keeps you full and satisfied, reducing the likelihood of overeating. Additionally, because the diet is balanced, it stabilizes blood sugar levels and reduces cravings, making it easier to maintain a healthy weight over time.

3. **Reduced Inflammation**:
   Chronic inflammation is a known factor in the development of many diseases, including arthritis, diabetes, and Alzheimer's. The Mediterranean diet is rich in anti-inflammatory foods, such as olive oil, fatty fish, nuts, and vegetables. The omega-3s in fish and the polyphenols in olive oil help to fight inflammation at a cellular level, promoting overall wellness and reducing the risk of chronic disease.

4. **Improved Longevity**:
   People in Mediterranean countries, particularly in regions like Sardinia and Ikaria, are known for their long lifespans. This is attributed in part to their traditional Mediterranean diet, which is rich in antioxidants, healthy fats, and nutrient-dense foods. Studies have found that following the Mediterranean diet can contribute to longer life expectancy and a better quality of life in older age.

5. **Brain Health**:
   There's growing evidence that the Mediterranean diet plays a key role in brain health. By reducing the risk of stroke and lowering levels of inflammation, it also helps preserve cognitive function. The high levels of antioxidants from fruits, vegetables, and olive oil protect brain cells from oxidative stress, and the omega-3s found in fish have been linked to improved memory and cognitive function, as well as a reduced risk of neurodegenerative diseases like Alzheimer's.

By understanding these core principles and the incredible health benefits they offer, you'll see that the Mediterranean diet is not just a passing trend but a sustainable, nourishing approach to eating. It's a way of life that embraces the joy of food, the pleasure of sharing meals with loved ones, and the commitment to long-term health.

THE MEDITERRANEAN LIFESTYLE

Chapter 2:

Regional Flavors and Dishes Across the Mediterranean

Exploring the Rich Diversity of Mediterranean Cuisines

The Mediterranean region is a melting pot of cultures, each contributing its own flavors, techniques, and culinary traditions. From the sun-drenched shores of Spain to the rich, fragrant spices of Morocco, Mediterranean cuisines are as diverse as the countries that surround the sea. While each region has its own distinct identity, they all share a common appreciation for fresh, seasonal ingredients, simple cooking methods, and bold flavors. Exploring Mediterranean cuisine means embarking on a culinary journey that takes you across borders, weaving together centuries of cultural exchange.

1. **The Southern European Influence**:
   Southern Europe—comprising Greece, Italy, and Spain—has long been the heart of Mediterranean cooking. The flavors of these countries are defined using olive oil, garlic, herbs, and tomatoes. Each country, however, puts its own unique spin on these ingredients. Italy's emphasis on pasta and risotto contrasts with Spain's love for rice-based dishes like paella and their famous tapas. Greece, on the other hand, incorporates a more pronounced use of lamb and yogurt, offering a robust and hearty flavor profile.
2. **North African Influence**:
   The Mediterranean diet also carries the flavors of North Africa, where aromatic spices, couscous, and tagine dishes reign supreme. Moroccan, Tunisian, and Algerian cuisines are characterized by bold flavors like cumin, coriander, cinnamon, and saffron. The influence of these spices, combined with the region's use of preserved foods like olives and dried fruits, brings a rich depth of flavor that's distinct from Southern Europe but no less beloved.
3. **Middle Eastern Fusion**:
   The Levant—comprising countries like Lebanon, Syria, and Turkey—introduces another layer of complexity to Mediterranean cuisine. Here, you'll find a mix of spices such as sumac, za'atar, and pomegranate molasses, with an emphasis on grilled meats, fresh salads, and yogurt-based sauces like tzatziki and labneh. The fusion of Middle Eastern

THE MEDITERRANEAN LIFESTYLE

and Mediterranean flavors creates a dynamic culinary tradition full of contrasts and bold tastes.

This chapter takes you on a sensory journey across these regions, celebrating their unique dishes while also highlighting the common threads that unite them: fresh ingredients, balanced flavors, and a focus on family and tradition.

The Tastes of Greece: From Souvlaki to Moussaka

Greece is a land where food is intertwined with culture, history, and community. From the Mediterranean's pristine coastlines to its mountainous regions, the Greek landscape offers an abundance of fresh ingredients that are essential to its cuisine. Greek food is vibrant and hearty, with a deep respect for tradition and the land.

1. **Souvlaki**:
   One of the most iconic Greek street foods, souvlaki is a simple yet flavorful dish of marinated meat, often lamb, chicken, or pork, skewered and grilled over an open flame. Served in a pita with fresh vegetables, a drizzle of tzatziki, and a sprinkle of herbs, souvlaki is the perfect embodiment of Greek culinary tradition—easy to make yet bursting with flavor. The marinade typically includes olive oil, lemon juice, garlic, and oregano, offering a perfect balance of savory, tangy, and herbal flavors.
2. **Moussaka**:
   Considered the national dish of Greece, moussaka is a comforting, layered casserole that combines eggplant, ground lamb (or beef), and béchamel sauce. It's the Greek equivalent of lasagna, with the eggplant replacing pasta sheets and the rich béchamel sauce offering a velvety, creamy texture that contrasts beautifully with the savory meat sauce beneath. This dish is a celebration of the Mediterranean's love for vegetables and meat, harmoniously layered together with fragrant spices like cinnamon, allspice, and nutmeg.
3. **Greek Salad (Horiatiki)**:
   A simple yet delightful dish, Greek salad captures the essence of Mediterranean eating. It typically consists of ripe tomatoes, cucumbers, red onions, Kalamata olives, and a large chunk of feta cheese, all drizzled with a generous amount of extra virgin olive oil and sprinkled with oregano. The beauty of Greek salad lies in its simplicity—the quality of the ingredients shines through in every bite, with the salty tang of feta, the crunch of fresh vegetables, and the rich olive oil bringing it all together.
4. **Spanakopita and Tirupati**:
   These flaky pastries are quintessential Greek comfort food. Spanakopita, a savory pie made with spinach, feta cheese, and phyllo dough, and tropia, which features a filling of feta and ricotta cheese, are popular throughout Greece. Whether served as a snack,

appetizer, or light meal, these pies are the epitome of Greek cuisine's balance between simplicity and indulgence.

5. **Baklava**:
No discussion of Greek cuisine would be complete without mentioning baklava—a rich, sweet pastry made from layers of phyllo dough, honey, and finely chopped nuts (usually pistachios or walnuts). The pastry is baked to golden perfection, and the sweetness of the honey syrup, combined with the crunch of the nuts, creates a delightful contrast in textures. Baklava is a true Mediterranean treat, enjoyed throughout Greece and the entire region, often served as a symbol of hospitality.

Greek cuisine offers a treasure trove of flavors and traditions, from the simple yet delicious street food of souvlaki to the hearty, layered complexity of moussaka. Whether it's a fresh Greek salad or a delicate pastry like baklava, every dish tells a story of the land, the people, and the Mediterranean way of life.

Spain's Best-Kept Secrets: Paella, Gazpacho, and Beyond

Spain offers a culinary treasure trove, brimming with vibrant flavors, rich textures, and a passion for sharing meals with family and friends. Spanish cuisine is famous for its regional diversity, with each area offering its own distinct dishes. But there are a few that stand out as iconic symbols of Spanish food culture.

1. **Paella**:
Perhaps the most famous of all Spanish dishes, paella originated in the region of Valencia. This saffron-infused rice dish, traditionally made with a variety of fresh seafood or chicken and rabbit, is cooked in a shallow pan to develop a crispy bottom layer, called the *Socarras*. Paella is not just a meal; it's a celebration of community. While there are many variations, from seafood paella to mixed versions, the dish's heart lies in its combination of rice, rich flavors, and aromatic spices.

2. **Gazpacho**:
A refreshing and revitalizing dish, gazpacho is the epitome of summer in Spain. This cold soup, typically made with tomatoes, cucumbers, bell peppers, garlic, olive oil, and vinegar, is both nutritious and hydrating—a perfect choice for hot Spanish afternoons. Originating from Andalusia, it combines the bounty of fresh vegetables with the tang of vinegar and the smoothness of olive oil, offering a perfect balance of flavors.

3. **Tapas**:
Tapas are small plates of food designed to be shared, offering a taste of everything from *patatas bravas* (crispy potatoes with spicy tomato sauce) to *jamun Iberica* (cured ham).

THE MEDITERRANEAN LIFESTYLE

These little bites highlight Spain's love of bold, punchy flavors and make for a social and fun dining experience.

Italy's Culinary Legacy: The Eternal Influence of Olive Oil, Pasta, and Pizza

Italy's culinary influence on the Mediterranean world cannot be overstated. From the rustic trattorias of Tuscany to the bustling streets of Naples, Italian cuisine has shaped the way people eat around the world. At the heart of Italy's cuisine are a few simple yet powerful ingredients—olive oil, pasta, and, of course, pizza.

1. **Olive Oil**:
   Italy is synonymous with olive oil, and for good reason. Italian olive oil, especially extra virgin olive oil, is not just an ingredient but a key player in almost every dish. Whether it's used as a base for sauces, drizzled over salads, or simply dipped with crusty bread, olive oil forms the foundation of Italian cooking. The rich, earthy flavor of high-quality olive oil is the hallmark of Italian cuisine and is seen as a symbol of both health and tradition.
2. **Pasta**:
   Italy's pasta culture is legendary. With hundreds of shapes and varieties, pasta has become the soul of Italian cuisine. From simple pasta dishes like *spaghetti agio e olio* (spaghetti with garlic and olive oil) to complex, regional specialties like *lasagna* or *pappardelle with wild boar ragu*, pasta is the cornerstone of Italy's culinary heritage. Italian chefs take great pride in using just a handful of ingredients—fresh pasta, tomatoes, garlic, basil, and cheese—to create iconic dishes that are beloved worldwide.
3. **Pizza**:
   It would be impossible to discuss Italian cuisine without mentioning pizza. Originating in Naples, the modern pizza is a brilliant combination of soft dough, rich tomato sauce, creamy mozzarella, and a variety of toppings. The classic *Margherita pizza*, with its vibrant red, white, and green colors, represents the colors of the Italian flag. But pizza in Italy varies regionally, from the thin-crust pizza of Rome to the thicker, doughier style found in the north.

North African Influences: Moroccan Tagine, Tunisian Couscous, and More

North Africa's culinary influence on Mediterranean cuisine is profound and undeniable. The rich, aromatic spices and techniques developed in Morocco, Tunisia, and other countries in the region have become an integral part of Mediterranean food culture.

THE MEDITERRANEAN LIFESTYLE

1. **Moroccan Tagine**:
   One of Morocco's most iconic dishes, tagine is a slow-cooked stew made in a traditional clay pot. The dish can include lamb, chicken, or beef, paired with vegetables, dried fruits, and a unique blend of spices like cumin, cinnamon, saffron, and ginger. The combination of sweet and savory flavors, often accentuated with a touch of honey or preserved lemons, makes tagine a deeply comforting and flavorful dish. The slow cooking process allows the ingredients to meld together, creating a rich and complex flavor profile.
2. **Tunisian Couscous**:
   Couscous is a staple throughout North Africa, but Tunisia takes it to a whole new level. Often served with a spicy tomato-based sauce, lamb, or vegetables, Tunisian couscous is a flavorful dish that can be adapted to any season or occasion. The distinctive flavors come from the use of harissa (a hot chili paste), olive oil, garlic, and a variety of aromatic spices, making it a hearty and satisfying meal.
3. **Spices and Sauces**:
   North African cuisine is marked by its bold use of spices—paprika, cumin, coriander, turmeric, and cinnamon are commonly used to infuse dishes with warmth and depth. Additionally, sauces like *chermoula* (a marinade made from herbs, garlic, lemon, and spices) and *harissa* (a spicy paste made from chili peppers and garlic) have influenced many Mediterranean chefs, adding a fiery edge to Mediterranean cuisine.

perfectly refreshing and nourishing, especially during the scorching summer months. Originating from the Andalusian region, gazpacho combines the ripest seasonal vegetables into a smooth, savory blend. It's often served chilled with optional garnishes like croutons, hard-boiled eggs, or finely chopped vegetables for added texture. This dish showcases the Mediterranean emphasis on fresh, seasonal ingredients and reflects Spain's knack for transforming simple produce into something extraordinary.

3. **Tapas**:
   Tapas are an iconic part of Spanish culture, a series of small dishes designed for sharing. They range from olives, cheeses, and cured meats to more elaborate offerings like *patatas bravas* (crispy fried potatoes with spicy tomato sauce) or *gambas al abilo* (garlic shrimp). Tapas are not just about food—they are about social connection and communal dining, turning meals into a festive experience where the food is meant to be shared and enjoyed with friends, family, and wine.
4. **Other Hidden Gems**:
   Beyond the well-known dishes, Spain's regional specialties offer endless surprises. In the Basque Country, *pintxos* (small snacks often served on skewers) dominate the bar scene. In the Canary Islands, *papas arribadas* (wrinkled potatoes) paired with a rich, spicy mojo sauce reflect the island's unique culinary heritage. Spain's cuisine invites you to explore its varied regions, each offering its own distinctive flavors and techniques.

THE MEDITERRANEAN LIFESTYLE

Italy's Culinary Legacy: The Eternal Influence of Olive Oil, Pasta, and Pizza

Italy is the birthplace of some of the world's most beloved foods. Its culinary legacy has influenced kitchens worldwide, and no matter where you are, the taste of Italian food is both comforting and universally recognized. But Italian cuisine is far more than just pasta and pizza—it's a celebration of the land's bounty, its regions, and centuries of culinary tradition.

1. **The Olive Oil Tradition**:
   At the heart of Italian cooking is olive oil—used generously in nearly every dish, from salads and pasta sauces to drizzling over freshly baked bread. The choice of olive oil is paramount, with extra virgin olive oil being the standard for high-quality flavor and health benefits. Its rich, grassy taste brings depth to Italian dishes, providing the base for sauces, dressings, and roasted vegetables.
2. **Pasta: The Ultimate Comfort Food**:
   Italy's love affair with pasta is legendary. With over 350 different shapes and varieties, pasta plays a central role in Italian meals. Each region of Italy has its own specialties, from the long strands of spaghetti in Naples to the stuffed *ravioli* in the north. Dishes like *pasta all carbonara, Bolognese,* and *pesto all Genovese* highlight the versatility of pasta, often paired with rich, slow-simmered sauces made from tomatoes, olive oil, garlic, and fresh herbs.
3. **Pizza: A Global Phenomenon**:
   Originally from Naples, pizza has become a global icon of Italian cuisine. The simplicity of a traditional Neapolitan pizza—thin, crisp crust topped with fresh mozzarella, basil, and tomatoes—reflects the essence of Mediterranean cooking. However, pizza has been embraced and adapted across Italy, with regional variations like *pizza al talion* in Rome or *pizza Bianca* (white pizza) found in central Italy.
4. **Regional Delights**:
   Italian cuisine is not monolithic—it is deeply regional, with each area offering unique dishes that reflect local agricultural practices and cultural influences. In the north, rich butter-based sauces and *risottos* define the cuisine, while in the south, Mediterranean staples like tomatoes, olives, and capers take center stage. The culinary diversity of Italy allows for endless exploration, whether it's enjoying *osso buco* in Milan, *arancini* in Sicily, or fresh seafood in coastal regions.

THE MEDITERRANEAN LIFESTYLE

North African Influences: Moroccan Tagine, Tunisian Couscous, and More

While the Mediterranean is often associated with Europe, the North African countries that border the sea—such as Morocco, Tunisia, and Algeria—offer a rich and aromatic culinary tradition that has deeply influenced Mediterranean cuisine.

1. **Moroccan Tagine**:
   Perhaps the most iconic North African dish, *tagine* is both the name of the pot in which the dish is cooked and the meal itself. This slow-cooked stew combines meats (often lamb, chicken, or beef) with vegetables, dried fruits like apricots or raisins, and a rich array of spices including cumin, cinnamon, ginger, and saffron. The result is a deeply flavorful dish, with tender meats and a complex, layered taste that's both sweet and savory. *Tagine* is often served with couscous or flatbread, which helps soak up the flavorful sauce.
2. **Tunisian Couscous**:
   Couscous is a staple in North Africa, and in Tunisia, it is often served as the base of a hearty stew. The couscous is steamed, then topped with a flavorful broth made from lamb, fish, or vegetables. What sets Tunisian couscous apart is its bold use of spices, such as harissa (a spicy chili paste), cumin, and coriander, which give the dish its signature heat and flavor.
3. **North African Spices**:
   The North African influence on Mediterranean cooking extends to its use of spices, which are often more aromatic and complex than in some European Mediterranean dishes. The use of spices like cumin, paprika, turmeric, cinnamon, and saffron lends a warm, earthy depth to dishes. Spice blends like *Ras ell hanout* (a mixture of spices) and *Baharat* are common in Moroccan cooking, adding a unique flair to tagines, stews, and even salads.
4. **Other Regional Delights**:
   In addition to couscous and tagine, North African cuisine is full of bold flavors and dishes that have left their mark on Mediterranean cuisine. In Tunisia, *Brik* (a pastry filled with egg and tuna) is a popular snack, while the use of preserved lemons and olives in many Moroccan dishes adds a distinctive tangy flavor. The influence of North Africa is also felt in Mediterranean salads, stews, and rice dishes, where the balance of fresh and preserved ingredients, along with the use of spices, creates memorable meals.

Italy's Culinary Legacy: The Eternal Influence of Olive Oil, Pasta, and Pizza

Italy, with its deeply rooted culinary traditions, is one of the most influential countries when it comes to Mediterranean cuisine. Italian cooking is characterized by its simplicity, allowing the natural flavors of fresh ingredients to shine. From the pasta-rich regions of the south to the

THE MEDITERRANEAN LIFESTYLE

seafood-laden coasts of the north, Italy's culinary legacy has spread worldwide, yet its roots remain deeply planted in the Mediterranean soil.

1. **Olive Oil**:
   Olive oil is not just an ingredient in Italian cooking; it's the foundation of the cuisine. Italy is home to some of the best olive oils in the world, particularly in regions like Tuscany and Puglia, where olive groves stretch across the hillsides. Extra virgin olive oil is used liberally in Italian kitchens, from drizzling over fresh salads to dressing pasta or sautéing vegetables. It adds a depth of flavor and richness to every dish, and its health benefits—such as its heart-healthy monounsaturated fats—are widely celebrated.

2. **Pasta**:
   Italian pasta is iconic, and the variety of shapes and styles available are endless. From *spaghetti* to *penne* to the regional favorites like *orecchiette* from Puglia or *cavatelli* from Calabria, pasta plays a starring role in almost every Italian meal. Each region has its own specialties, often paired with locally sourced ingredients like fresh tomatoes, basil, ricotta, and a variety of meats and seafood. The balance of pasta with rich, aromatic sauces—whether a simple tomato sauce or a more decadent ragù—shows Italy's commitment to quality, flavor, and balance.

3. **Pizza**:
   No discussion of Italian cuisine would be complete without pizza. Originating from Naples, pizza has become one of the world's most beloved dishes. The traditional *Margherita* pizza, with its thin crust, fresh mozzarella, tomatoes, and basil, embodies the perfect harmony of flavors. While pizza has evolved in many places across the globe, the Neapolitan version remains the gold standard. Italy's pizza tradition, rooted in simplicity, highlights the quality of its ingredients—from the delicate mozzarella di bufala to the tangy San Marzano tomatoes.

4. **Other Italian Delights**:
   Beyond pasta and pizza, Italy is home to a wide variety of regional specialties. In the north, risottos and polenta dominate the plate, with the use of butter and cream offering a rich contrast to the olive oil-based dishes of the south. The island of Sicily offers sweet treats like cannoli and granita, while the regions of Emilia-Romagna and Piedmont are known for rich, luxurious dishes like *lasagna* and *agio e olio* pasta. Each dish tells a story, passed down through generations and perfected with time.

North African Influences: Moroccan Tagine, Tunisian Couscous, and More

North African cuisine, particularly from countries like Morocco, Tunisia, and Algeria, has made a profound impact on the Mediterranean diet, adding complexity and depth using aromatic spices and slow-cooked dishes. The influence of North African flavors is felt not only in the southern

THE MEDITERRANEAN LIFESTYLE

Mediterranean but also in parts of Spain and France, where ingredients like cumin, coriander, saffron, and cinnamon have woven their way into local cuisines.

1. **Moroccan Tagine**:
   Tagine is a hallmark of Moroccan cuisine—slow-cooked stews made in a special clay pot of the same name. These dishes typically feature a combination of meats (lamb, chicken), vegetables, dried fruits (apricots, raisins), and nuts (almonds), all stewed together with fragrant spices like cumin, cinnamon, and saffron. The result is a dish that balances savory and sweet flavors, with layers of complexity that are a hallmark of Moroccan cooking. Tagines are often paired with *couscous*, another staple of North African cuisine.

2. **Tunisian Couscous**:
   Couscous, while often associated with Mediterranean and Middle Eastern cuisines, is a mainstay of North African cooking. In Tunisia, couscous is often served with lamb, chicken, or vegetables, and cooked in a flavorful broth rich with spices like harissa (a spicy chili paste) and coriander. This dish represents the depth and heat of Tunisian cuisine, where bold flavors are embraced. Couscous is also a popular dish in other parts of North Africa, served with stews or grilled meats.

3. **Spices and Herbs**:
   The spice profile in North African cuisine is another area that sets it apart from Southern European Mediterranean dishes. North African cooks rely on a rich palette of spices like cumin, turmeric, paprika, saffron, and cinnamon. These spices not only create depth in flavor but also offer numerous health benefits, such as anti-inflammatory properties and digestive support. In Tunisia, for example, the use of harissa—spicy and aromatic—is a staple in many dishes, giving them an unmistakable heat and complexity.

4. **Other North African Influences**:
   Beyond couscous and tagine, North African cuisine features a variety of other dishes like *pastilla* (a sweet-savory pastry often filled with pigeon or chicken), *mechanic* (slow-roasted lamb), and *briquets* (fried pastries filled with savory fillings like cheese or spiced meat). North African food is a perfect example of how food, culture, and geography intersect to create a vibrant and unique culinary tradition that continues to influence Mediterranean eating.

THE MEDITERRANEAN LIFESTYLE

Chapter 3:

Key Mediterranean Ingredients and How to Use Them

Olive Oil, Herbs, and Spices: The Foundations of Mediterranean Flavor

At the heart of Mediterranean cuisine is a handful of ingredients that serve as the building blocks for the bold, fragrant, and deeply satisfying flavors found in its dishes. Olive oil, herbs, and spices not only define the Mediterranean diet but also embody its essence: fresh, natural, and aromatic.

1. **Olive Oil**:
   Olive oil is more than just a cooking fat in the Mediterranean; it is an essential ingredient used in almost every dish, from salad dressings to stews and even desserts. The best olive oils are cold-pressed, unrefined, and full of flavor. Extra virgin olive oil is prized for its rich, fruity taste and health benefits. It's often used as a finishing touch, drizzled over roasted vegetables, grilled fish, or pasta dishes to enhance their flavor. The importance of olive oil in Mediterranean cuisine cannot be overstated—it's the golden elixir that brings together the flavors of the region.
2. **Herbs**:
   Mediterranean herbs are aromatic and plentiful, playing a central role in shaping the flavors of the region's cuisine. Some of the most used herbs include:
   - **Basil**: A key player in Italian cooking, especially in pesto and tomato-based dishes.
   - **Oregano**: Used in Greek and Italian dishes, it pairs beautifully with meats, vegetables, and tomato sauces.
   - **Thyme**: This herb is versatile, used in everything from Mediterranean roasts to stews and marinades.
   - **Rosemary**: Especially popular in southern Italy and Greece, rosemary's robust flavor complements lamb, chicken, and potatoes.
3. **Spices**:
   Spices in the Mediterranean are varied but generally subtle, meant to enhance rather than overpower dishes. Common spices include:

- **Saffron**: Often used in paella or risotto, saffron lends a delicate floral flavor and vibrant yellow color to dishes.
- **Cumin**: Found in North African and Middle Eastern cooking, cumin adds warmth and depth to tagines, couscous, and lentil dishes.
- **Paprika**: Essential in Spanish dishes, especially in *pistol* (a vegetable stew) and *patatas bravas* (fried potatoes with spicy tomato sauce).
- **Cinnamon**: Used in both sweet and savory dishes, cinnamon is integral to Moroccan stews and desserts.

The Mediterranean Pantry: Must-Have Ingredients for Every Kitchen

To cook Mediterranean food at home, certain ingredients will become your staples. These pantry essentials are versatile and store well, allowing you to create a wide array of Mediterranean dishes with ease.

1. **Canned Tomatoes**:
   Tomatoes are the backbone of Mediterranean cooking. While fresh tomatoes are ideal, canned tomatoes are an indispensable pantry item. They are perfect for sauces, soups, and stews, providing rich flavor and texture. San Marzano tomatoes are highly prized for their sweet flavor and low acidity, especially in Italian dishes.
2. **Legumes and Beans**:
   Beans and legumes are a key source of protein and are widely used across the Mediterranean. Whether it's chickpeas for making hummus, lentils for soups, or white beans in stews, these pantry staples are the heart of many vegetarian Mediterranean dishes. They also provide fiber, making them a nutritious and filling addition to any meal.
3. **Rice and Grains**:
   The Mediterranean boasts a variety of grains and rice used in everything from pilafs to risottos. Some essential grains include:
   - **Arborio Rice**: Used in creamy risottos, especially in Italy.
   - **Couscous**: A staple in North African cuisine, couscous is perfect for soaking up rich stews and tagines.
   - **Farro**: A whole grain used in Italian salads and soups, farro has a nutty flavor and chewy texture.
   - **Bulgur Wheat**: Often used in Middle Eastern dishes like tabbouleh, bulgur is an easy-to-prepare whole grain packed with fiber and protein.
4. **Nuts and Seeds**:
   Nuts and seeds play an important role in Mediterranean cooking, adding both texture and

flavor. They are often used in sauces, salads, and baked goods. Almonds, pine nuts, and walnuts are especially common in both savory and sweet dishes. Pine nuts, for example, are essential in pesto, while almonds are used in a variety of Italian desserts like *torta di mandrel* (almond cake).

5. **Cheese**:
   Mediterranean cheeses, with their rich, salty flavors, are integral to many dishes. Some popular ones include:
   - **Feta**: A crumbly, briny cheese from Greece, perfect in salads, pastries, or as a topping for roasted vegetables.
   - **Parmesan**: Known as *Parmigiano-Reggiano*, this aged, hard cheese from Italy is essential in pasta dishes, risottos, and soups.
   - **Ricotta**: A soft cheese that adds creaminess to both savory and sweet Italian dishes, including lasagna, ravioli, and cheesecakes.

Fresh Produce and Seafood: Seasonal and Local Ingredients that Define the Region

One of the key characteristics of Mediterranean cuisine is its reliance on fresh, seasonal produce, much of which is grown in the fertile soil of the Mediterranean region. Vegetables, fruits, and seafood are not just ingredients; they are the stars of the show.

1. **Fresh Vegetables**:
   Vegetables like tomatoes, bell peppers, eggplants, zucchini, and cucumbers feature prominently in Mediterranean dishes. In fact, the Mediterranean diet is often called a "vegetable-first" approach to cooking. Vegetables are used in stews, salads, pastas, and even as stand-alone dishes, prepared simply with olive oil, garlic, and fresh herbs. In Greece, *bream* (a roasted vegetable medley) is a beloved dish that showcases the region's love for seasonal produce.

2. **Fruits**:
   Mediterranean fruits, such as citrus fruits (lemons, oranges, and grapefruits), figs, pomegranates, and grapes, are used both in savory dishes and for desserts. Figs, for example, are a key ingredient in both savory Moroccan tagines and sweet Italian pastries. Pomegranate seeds add a burst of freshness to salads and couscous dishes, while citrus zest and juice are used to brighten up everything from seafood to desserts.

3. **Seafood**:
   With the Mediterranean Sea surrounding the region, seafood is a fundamental part of the diet. Fish like anchovies, sardines, and mackerel are commonly grilled or marinated. Shellfish, such as shrimp, octopus, and mussels, are often found in paella, pasta dishes, or

seafood stews. Seafood in the Mediterranean is typically simple, prepared with just a touch of olive oil, garlic, and fresh herbs, allowing the natural flavors to shine through.

flavors of Mediterranean cooking. Common herbs like **oregano**, **basil**, **rosemary**, **thyme**, and **mint** are used liberally, each adding its own distinct layer of fragrance and depth. Fresh herbs are often added at the end of cooking to preserve their vibrant aromas, though dried herbs are also common, especially in slow-cooked dishes. For instance, **oregano** is a must-have in Greek cuisine, flavoring everything from **Greek salads** to **souvlaki**, while **rosemary** is frequently paired with roasted meats and potatoes in Italy and Spain.

4. **Spices**:
   The Mediterranean may not be as spice laden as other parts of the world, but the use of select spices elevates the cuisine to new heights. **Saffron**, with its deep golden color and floral flavor, is especially prized in dishes like **paella** and **risotto**. **Cumin** and **coriander** add warm, earthy notes to North African tagines and stews. **Paprika** is another spice commonly used, especially in Spanish and Hungarian dishes, to add both color and a subtle smokiness. **Cinnamon** and **cloves** are used in more sweet-and-savory combinations, as seen in Middle Eastern dishes like **lamb tagine** with dried fruits.

The Mediterranean Pantry: Must-Have Ingredients for Every Kitchen

A well-stocked Mediterranean pantry is the foundation of any great Mediterranean meal. These pantry staples are versatile, long-lasting, and can transform a simple dish into something extraordinary. Here's a rundown of the must-have ingredients that should be in every Mediterranean kitchen:

1. **Olives and Olive Products**:
   Olives are a staple of Mediterranean diets, not just eaten whole, but also incorporated into oils, pastes, and tapenade. **Green olives** tend to be milder, while **black olives** are richer and more intensely flavored. **Olive paste** or **tapenade** is a blend of olives, capers, and olive oil, perfect for spreading on bread or adding to pasta dishes.
2. **Legumes and Beans**:
   Beans, lentils, and chickpeas are at the heart of Mediterranean cooking. Rich in protein and fiber, they serve as a healthy base for soups, stews, and salads. Classic dishes like **hummus, falafel,** and **caponata** all rely on these versatile ingredients.
3. **Grains**:
   Couscous, bulgur wheat, and **quinoa** are essential grains that pair perfectly with roasted vegetables, stews, or grilled meats. **Rice**—particularly the short-grain variety like **arborio**—is another important pantry item, often found in risottos and paella.

THE MEDITERRANEAN LIFESTYLE

4. **Nuts and Seeds**:
   Mediterranean cuisine incorporates a wide variety of nuts and seeds, such as **almonds**, **pine nuts**, and **pistachios**. These add texture and richness to both savory and sweet dishes. **Tahini**—a paste made from ground sesame seeds—is a fundamental ingredient in Middle Eastern dips and sauces, while **pine nuts** lend a delicate crunch to **pesto** and Mediterranean salads.

5. **Tomatoes**:
   Fresh, ripe tomatoes are a staple in Mediterranean kitchens, used in everything from sauces to salads. **Sun-dried tomatoes** are also a pantry essential, providing intense flavor in pasta dishes, pizzas, and Mediterranean sandwiches.

Fresh Produce and Seafood: Seasonal and Local Ingredients that Define the Region

One of the most distinctive features of Mediterranean cooking is its reliance on seasonal, local produce and seafood. The Mediterranean Sea itself provides an abundant source of fish and shellfish, while the region's climate fosters a variety of fruits and vegetables that define the cuisine.

1. **Fresh Produce**:
   Mediterranean cuisine shines with the use of seasonal produce, which varies depending on the region and time of year. **Tomatoes, eggplants, zucchini, peppers**, and **cucumbers** are the backbone of many Mediterranean salads and vegetable dishes. **Leafy greens** like **spinach, arugula**, and **chard** make regular appearances in salads, pastas, and stews. Citrus fruits, such as **lemons, oranges**, and **grapefruits**, are widely used for their refreshing acidity, which balances the richness of meats and adds brightness to seafood dishes.

2. **Seafood**:
   Being surrounded by water, seafood is a fundamental part of Mediterranean cuisine. From the crystal-clear waters of the Aegean to the fish-rich coasts of Spain and Italy, the Mediterranean is a bounty of fresh fish and shellfish. **Anchovies, sardines, octopus, squid**, and **scallops** are staples in Mediterranean diets, often grilled, roasted, or used in stews and pastas. **Fresh fish**, such as **branzino** (Mediterranean bass) or **dorado** (sea bream), are perfect when simply grilled with olive oil, lemon, and herbs.

3. **Herbs and Vegetables**:
   Mediterranean vegetables and herbs are vibrant and fragrant, contributing not only flavor but also color and texture. **Artichokes, fennel, onions**, and **garlic** form the base of many dishes, while herbs like **parsley, dill**, and **oregano** elevate the flavors of everything they touch. Whether fresh or dried, herbs play a key role in Mediterranean cuisine, offering freshness in salads and depth in slow-cooked dishes.

THE MEDITERRANEAN LIFESTYLE

are often used in Moroccan and Tunisian cooking, adding depth to savory stews and aromatic rice dishes. The careful balance of these herbs and spices—often used sparingly but thoughtfully—creates the signature flavor profiles that are so distinctive to Mediterranean cuisine. Whether used to season grilled meats, flavor rice dishes, or infuse stews, these spices work in harmony with the natural ingredients, amplifying their flavors without overwhelming them.

The Mediterranean Pantry: Must-Have Ingredients for Every Kitchen

A well-stocked Mediterranean pantry is the key to easily crafting flavorful dishes at home. These essential ingredients are the foundation of the Mediterranean diet, allowing you to prepare a wide variety of meals, from light salads to hearty stews. Here are some pantry staples that every Mediterranean kitchen should have:

1. **Legumes and Pulses**:
   Beans, lentils, and chickpeas are the cornerstone of Mediterranean vegetarian cooking. **Chickpeas** are used in everything from **hummus** to **falafel**, while **lentils** make their way into soups, stews, and salads. **Cannellini beans** are popular in Italian cooking, often added to hearty **minestrone soups** or served with roasted vegetables.
2. **Grains and Pasta**:
   Whole grains like farro, barley, and bulgur are staples in Mediterranean diets, providing a healthy, fiber-rich base for many dishes. **Couscous**, a staple in North Africa, is another versatile grain often used as a side dish or in salads. **Pasta** is, of course, a cornerstone of Italian cuisine, available in countless shapes and sizes. In many Mediterranean kitchens, pasta is paired with fresh vegetables, seafood, or simple sauces made from olive oil, garlic, and herbs.
3. **Tomatoes and Tomato Products**:
   Fresh, sun-ripened **tomatoes** are a fundamental part of Mediterranean cuisine, but **tomato paste**, **canned tomatoes**, and **passata** (tomato purée) are also pantry essentials. These ingredients form the base for a variety of sauces, from the **tomato-based sauces** that accompany pasta in Italy to the rich, spiced **tomato sauces** that are used in stews and tagines in North Africa.
4. **Nuts and Seeds**:
   Almonds, **pistachios**, and **walnuts** are commonly used in Mediterranean cooking, both in savory and sweet dishes. In Greece, for instance, **pistachios** are often used in pastries like **baklava**, while **almonds** add a subtle crunch to dishes like **hummus** and Mediterranean salads. **Sesame seeds** and **tahini** are also crucial in Mediterranean kitchens, forming the base of sauces and dips like **hummus** and **baba ghanoush**.

THE MEDITERRANEAN LIFESTYLE

5. **Vinegar and Wine**:
   Red wine vinegar, **balsamic vinegar**, and **sherry vinegar** are common in Mediterranean kitchens, providing a tangy, acidic balance to rich, olive oil-based dishes. **Wine**—especially white wine—is used in many Mediterranean dishes for deglazing, braising, and adding depth of flavor to sauces and stews.

Fresh Produce and Seafood: Seasonal and Local Ingredients that Define the Region

One of the core principles of Mediterranean cooking is the use of fresh, seasonal, and local produce. The Mediterranean climate, with its hot, dry summers and mild winters, allows for a rich bounty of fruits, vegetables, and herbs throughout the year.

1. **Fresh Vegetables**:
   Vegetables form the backbone of the Mediterranean diet, and they are often the stars of the plate. **Tomatoes**, **eggplants**, **zucchini**, **peppers**, and **onions** are some of the most common vegetables used in Mediterranean cooking. **Spinach**, **kale**, and other leafy greens are essential in salads and cooked dishes, while **artichokes**, **fennel**, and **asparagus** make appearances in more seasonal recipes.
2. **Fruits**:
   The Mediterranean is known for its variety of fruits, both common and exotic. **Citrus fruits** such as lemons and oranges are used extensively in cooking, adding brightness to dishes or being used for zest in dressings and marinades. **Figs, grapes, pomegranates**, and **apples** are frequently found in desserts, salads, and savory stews, showcasing the region's ability to combine sweet and savory flavors. **Olives**, another Mediterranean staple, are used both as an ingredient in dishes and enjoyed as snacks or appetizers, often marinated in olive oil, garlic, and herbs.
3. **Seafood**:
   With its extensive coastline, the Mediterranean region is home to some of the best seafood in the world. Fresh, sustainable **fish**like **sardines**, **anchovies**, and **bream** are often grilled or roasted whole, preserving their natural flavor. **Shellfish**—such as **mussels, clams, shrimp**, and **lobster**—are also common and used in a variety of dishes, from **paella** to **seafood stews**. **Octopus** and **squid** are celebrated in Mediterranean countries like Greece and Spain, often grilled or braised in flavorful sauces.

THE MEDITERRANEAN LIFESTYLE

Chapter 4:

Mediterranean Cooking Techniques

Slow-Cooked Delights: Stews, Roasts, and Braises

One of the defining characteristics of Mediterranean cuisine is the art of slow cooking. Whether simmering a rich **lamb stew** in Morocco or slowly roasting a **pork shoulder** in Spain, the Mediterranean way of slow cooking allows the ingredients to meld together, developing deep, complex flavors that are both comforting and satisfying.

1. **Stews and Braises**:
   Mediterranean stews and braises are often made with a combination of tender meats, vegetables, and aromatic herbs, cooked over low heat for hours. Dishes like **tagine** (a slow-cooked Moroccan stew) or **moussaka** (a layered Greek casserole) rely on long cooking times to tenderize tougher cuts of meat and allow the flavors to blend beautifully. The key to successful slow-cooking is patience—by taking your time, you allow the natural flavors of the ingredients to fully emerge, resulting in rich, hearty dishes that are perfect for family meals or entertainment.
2. **Roasting**:
   Roasting is another technique that takes full advantage of the Mediterranean's abundance of fresh produce. Roasted **vegetables**, like zucchini, eggplant, tomatoes, and bell peppers, are a common side dish in Mediterranean cooking, often drizzled with olive oil and sprinkled with herbs like **rosemary** and **thyme**. Roasting intensifies the natural sweetness of vegetables and enhances their texture. **Roast lamb**, **chicken**, or **fish** is also a staple in many Mediterranean countries, with spices and herbs acting as a flavoring agent to elevate the dish.
3. **Braising**:
   Braising is a technique where food is browned in fat and then cooked slowly in a small amount of liquid. It is commonly used for tougher cuts of meat like **beef shank**, **lamb shoulder**, or **chicken thighs**. Braised dishes like **osso buco** (Italian braised veal shanks) or **chicken with olives** (a Greek specialty) are tender, flavorful, and perfect for soaking up the aromas of herbs, spices, and broths.

THE MEDITERRANEAN LIFESTYLE

Grilling and Barbecuing: The Mediterranean Love for Charred Flavor

Grilling and barbecuing are quintessential Mediterranean techniques, particularly in countries like Greece, Spain, and Turkey, where the joy of cooking over an open flame is as much about the experience as it is about the food. The smoky, charred flavors that come from grilling enhance the natural sweetness of vegetables, seafood, and meats, creating a bold and unforgettable taste.

1. **Grilled Meats**:
   Souvlaki (Greek skewered meat), **chicken shawarma** (Middle Eastern spiced chicken), and **lamb kebabs** are some of the most popular Mediterranean grilled dishes. The key to perfect grilling is marinating your meats beforehand to tenderize them and infuse them with aromatic flavors. Mediterranean marinades typically include ingredients like **olive oil**, **garlic**, **lemon juice**, **oregano**, and **cumin**, which not only tenderize but also impart deep flavor.
2. **Grilled Seafood**:
   The Mediterranean Sea is abundant in fresh fish and seafood, and grilling is one of the best ways to bring out their natural flavor. **Grilled sardines**, **sea bass**, and **octopus** are commonly found on Mediterranean grills. The fish is often simply seasoned with **olive oil**, **lemon**, and **herbs** like **thyme** or **oregano**. Grilled octopus—charred on the outside while tender inside—is a beloved dish in Greece and Spain, served with a drizzle of olive oil and a squeeze of lemon.
3. **Vegetables on the Grill**:
   Vegetables, too, benefit from grilling. **Eggplant, zucchini, bell peppers**, and **asparagus** are often grilled, either whole or sliced, and then dressed with olive oil and herbs. The slight char enhances their natural flavors, making them ideal as side dishes or even main course components when served with a grain or protein.
4. **Barbecuing**:
   Mediterranean barbecuing often refers to cooking over an open flame or charcoal grill, particularly for larger cuts of meat. Barbecued **lamb** or **whole fish** is a signature feature in countries like Greece and Turkey. The slow cooking process over wood or coals infuses the food with a smoky depth that is simply unmatched by other methods.

Simple, Elegant Sauces: Dressings, Dips, and Drizzles

The beauty of Mediterranean cooking lies in its ability to take basic ingredients and elevate them with minimal effort. Sauces, dressings, and dips are the perfect example of this simplicity. These

THE MEDITERRANEAN LIFESTYLE

condiments not only enhance the flavor of the dishes they accompany but also serve as a vehicle for showcasing fresh, high-quality ingredients.

1. **Dressings**:
   Mediterranean salads, such as the famous **Greek salad**, are typically dressed with **extra virgin olive oil, lemon juice, vinegar**, and **herbs**. The dressing is simple, but the quality of the olive oil makes all the difference. In Italy, **balsamic vinegar** and **olive oil** are often combined for a rich, slightly tangy dressing, perfect for drizzling over fresh tomatoes or **mozzarella di bufala**. The beauty of Mediterranean dressings is in their simplicity—just a few ingredients, combined in the right proportions, create a deliciously fresh and vibrant result.

2. **Dips**:
   Mediterranean dips are staples at gatherings, whether it's **hummus** from the Middle East, **tzatziki** from Greece, or **baba ghanoush** from Lebanon. These dips often feature ingredients like **garlic, yogurt, olive oil, tahini**, and **lemon**, which are blended to create rich, flavorful spreads. **Hummus**, for example, is made from **chickpeas, garlic, tahini**, and **lemon juice**, and is typically served with warm pita bread or fresh vegetables. The smooth texture of these dips, combined with their bold, earthy flavors, makes them perfect for serving as appetizers or accompaniments to grilled meats and vegetables.

3. **Drizzles**:
   A simple drizzle of high-quality **extra virgin olive oil** is often all it takes to elevate a dish. Whether over **roasted vegetables, pasta**, or **grilled fish**, the olive oil enhances the flavors and adds richness. Another classic drizzle is **tahini sauce**, often paired with **falafel** or **grilled meats**, which adds a creamy texture and nutty depth. **Pomegranate molasses** is another favorite drizzle in Middle Eastern and North African cuisines, adding a sweet and tart note to stews, salads, and grilled dishes.

Vegetables, especially **eggplant, zucchini, bell peppers**, and **tomatoes**, are a hallmark of Mediterranean cooking. Roasting brings out their natural sweetness, intensifying their flavors and creating a caramelized, slightly crispy texture. In Mediterranean roasts, ingredients like **garlic, herbs** (such as **rosemary** and **thyme**), and a drizzle of **olive oil** are often used to enhance the vegetables' natural flavors. Meats, such as **lamb, chicken**, or **pork**, are also commonly roasted, often marinated with a combination of Mediterranean herbs, garlic, and citrus before being placed in the oven for hours, ensuring tenderness and a deep, savory flavor.

The Mediterranean approach to slow cooking is all about coaxing the best out of the ingredients, using low heat to achieve dishes that are tender, juicy, and packed with layers of flavor.

Grilling and Barbecuing: The Mediterranean Love for Charred Flavor

THE MEDITERRANEAN LIFESTYLE

In Mediterranean cultures, grilling is not just a cooking technique—it's a way of life. Grilled food carries a rich, smoky flavor that is quintessential to the Mediterranean experience. Whether it's **grilled fish** by the coast of Greece, **souvlaki** skewers in Turkey, or a **whole lamb** roasted over an open fire in Morocco, grilling is one of the most iconic and beloved cooking methods across the region.

1. **The Grill as a Social Experience**:
   In many Mediterranean cultures, grilling is a communal activity. **Barbecues** (or **asados**, as they are known in Spain) are often family affairs, where food is cooked over an open flame, accompanied by lively conversation, music, and shared laughter. The grill, whether it's a traditional **charcoal** or a modern **gas grill**, provides a unique way to bring people together. Grilled food is often served with an assortment of **dips**, **salads**, and **flatbreads**, turning the meal into a feast that is more than just food—it's an experience.
2. **Perfectly Grilled Proteins**:
   Mediterranean grilling is known for its simplicity—often, just a little **olive oil**, **garlic**, **lemon**, and **herbs** are used to marinate the meat. The key is to allow the flavors to shine without overpowering the natural taste of the protein. Grilled **fish**, such as **sardines** or **mackerel**, is incredibly popular in coastal Mediterranean countries, as is **chicken**, **lamb**, and **beef**. The high heat of the grill creates a crispy, charred exterior while keeping the interior juicy and tender.
3. **Vegetables on the Grill**:
   Vegetables are also a star on the grill. **Peppers**, **eggplants**, **onions**, and **tomatoes**—sometimes brushed with a bit of **olive oil** and sprinkled with **sea salt**—become deliciously smoky and tender. These grilled vegetables are often served as side dishes or used in salads like **Greek salad**, where the charred flavors complement the freshness of the raw vegetables.

Simple, Elegant Sauces: Dressings, Dips, and Drizzles

One of the best aspects of Mediterranean cooking is its ability to create extraordinary dishes with minimal ingredients. The secret often lies in the sauces—simple, yet powerful dressings, dips, and drizzles that elevate everything they touch. These sauces add flavor, richness, and a touch of elegance to even the simplest of meals.

1. **Dressings and Vinaigrettes**:
   Olive oil forms the base of many Mediterranean dressings, often paired with **vinegar** (usually **red wine** or **balsamic**), **mustard**, or **lemon juice**. A traditional **Greek salad dressing** is made with extra virgin olive oil, red wine vinegar, oregano, garlic, and a

pinch of salt and pepper. The result is a light, zesty dressing that enhances the flavors of fresh vegetables, grilled meats, or seafood.

2. **Dips**:

   Dips are a key element of Mediterranean appetizers, perfect for snacking or sharing with friends and family. **Hummus**—a blend of **chickpeas, tahini, garlic, lemon juice,** and **olive oil**—is a staple throughout the region, especially in countries like Lebanon, Israel, and Palestine. It's creamy, rich, and comforting, often served with **pita bread** or fresh vegetables. Another popular dip is **tzatziki**, a refreshing Greek yogurt-based dip with **cucumber, garlic, dill,** and **lemon juice**. It pairs wonderfully with grilled meats, flatbreads, or as a side dish.

3. **Salsas and Relishes**:

   Mediterranean countries also feature a variety of fresh salsas and relishes to serve alongside grilled meats and seafood. **Salsa Verde** from Italy, made with **parsley, garlic, capers,** and **olive oil**, is often drizzled over grilled fish or lamb. **Chermoula**, a North African sauce made with **cilantro, garlic, spices,** and **olive oil**, is used as a marinade or accompaniment to grill fish, offering a vibrant, tangy kick.

4. **Drizzles**:

   Mediterranean chefs often drizzle **extra virgin olive oil** over cooked dishes to finish them, enhancing the flavor and adding a silky richness. A drizzle of **lemon juice** or **balsamic glaze** can add a final touch of acidity and sweetness to roasted vegetables, grilled meats, or pasta dishes, bringing balance and complexity to the plate.

THE MEDITERRANEAN LIFESTYLE

Chapter 5:

Breakfasts and Brunches

Mediterranean Morning Delights: Frittatas, Yogurts, and Pastries

Breakfast in the Mediterranean is typically light, fresh, and wholesome, offering a perfect balance of protein, healthy fats, and vibrant flavors. The Mediterranean morning meal is often enjoyed slowly, accompanied by a coffee or herbal tea, and sometimes shared with family or friends, making it both nourishing and communal.

1. **Frittatas**:
   One of the staples of a Mediterranean breakfast, the **frittata** is a versatile, egg-based dish that can be loaded with a variety of ingredients. Think of it as a fluffy, Italian-style omelet, often filled with seasonal vegetables, herbs, and cheeses. A classic **Italian frittata** might feature **zucchini, tomatoes,** and **fresh basil**, while in Greece, **spinach** and **feta** come together in the popular **spanakopita** frittata. The beauty of a frittata is that it can be made ahead of time and served hot or at room temperature, making it a great choice for brunch or a quick, satisfying breakfast.
2. **Greek Yogurt**:
   No Mediterranean breakfast is complete without a serving of **Greek yogurt**, which is thicker and creamier than regular yogurt. Often topped with honey, fresh fruit, and a sprinkle of nuts, Greek yogurt is the epitome of Mediterranean simplicity and indulgence. It's rich in protein and probiotics, offering a wholesome start to the day. For a savories twist, Greek yogurt can be paired with olive oil, herbs, and a pinch of sea salt, creating a refreshing dip or side dish to enjoy with whole-grain bread or vegetables.
3. **Pastries**:
   While not always a daily occurrence, pastries are an important part of Mediterranean breakfasts, particularly in countries like **Turkey** and **France**. In **Turkey**, the famous **börek**, a savory pastry filled with cheese, spinach, or minced meat, is often eaten for breakfast, along with olives and fresh bread. In **France, croissants** or **pain au chocolate** are the epitome of indulgence, usually enjoyed with a café au lait. Mediterranean pastries

THE MEDITERRANEAN LIFESTYLE

tend to be less sweet than their American counterparts, often using natural ingredients like **olive oil** and **nuts** to create textures that are both rich and delicate.

Fresh and Hearty Starts to Your Day: Mediterranean-Inspired Smoothies, Toasts, and More

For those looking for a lighter, more portable breakfast option, the Mediterranean also offers plenty of fresh and hearty ideas. With an emphasis on seasonal fruits, vegetables, and whole grains, these breakfast options are both satisfying and nourishing.

1. **Mediterranean Smoothies**:
   Mediterranean-inspired smoothies are a blend of nutrient-dense fruits, vegetables, and healthy fats, making them perfect for a quick yet satisfying breakfast. A typical Mediterranean smoothie might feature ingredients like **Greek yogurt**, **citrus fruits** (such as oranges or grapefruits), and **leafy greens** like **spinach** or **kale**. Adding a spoonful of **tahini** or **almond butter** provides a creamy texture and healthy fats, while **olive oil** can add richness and a subtle earthy flavor. The Mediterranean approach to smoothies emphasizes whole, natural ingredients that provide long-lasting energy throughout the morning.

2. **Avocado Toast**:
   While **avocado toast** may have gained popularity worldwide in recent years, it has Mediterranean roots. The use of **avocado**, paired with whole-grain **bread** (a staple in many Mediterranean countries), makes for a delicious and nutritious breakfast option. Top your avocado toast with a drizzle of **extra virgin olive oil**, a sprinkle of **sea salt**, and a dash of **lemon juice** for a refreshing Mediterranean twist. You can also add toppings like **tomato slices**, **feta cheese**, or a soft-boiled egg to make it heartier and satisfying.

3. **Whole-Grain Toast with Tomato and Olive Oil**:
   Another classic Mediterranean breakfast, particularly in Spain and Italy, is a simple yet flavorful **tomato toast**. Made by rubbing ripe **tomatoes** on toasted **whole-grain bread**, this dish is often finished with a generous drizzle of **olive oil** and a pinch of **sea salt**. For added richness, you can top it with a slice of **mozzarella** or a sprinkle of **oregano**. This fresh, savory breakfast is quick to prepare but packed with nutrients—thanks to the healthy fats in olive oil and the antioxidants in the tomatoes.

4. **Chia Pudding**:
   Chia seeds, though not native to the Mediterranean, are becoming increasingly popular due to their high content of omega-3 fatty acids, fiber, and protein. When soaked in **almond milk** or **Greek yogurt**, chia seeds create a creamy, pudding-like consistency that can be eaten as a breakfast or a snack. Mediterranean-inspired chia pudding can be

topped with a variety of fresh fruits, such as **berries**, **figs**, or **pomegranate seeds**, as well as a drizzle of **honey** and a handful of **almonds** for extra texture.

Greek Yogurt with Honey and Nuts:
Greek yogurt is another breakfast favorite that is as versatile as it is delicious. Known for its thick, creamy texture and rich, tangy flavor, Greek yogurt serves as the base for many Mediterranean breakfasts. Often, it is topped with **local honey**, **crushed nuts**, and **fresh fruit**. The natural sweetness of honey pairs perfectly with the tartness of the yogurt, while nuts like **walnuts** or **almonds** provide a crunchy texture and a boost of healthy fats. In many Mediterranean countries, this simple dish is a go-to breakfast for its nutritional value and satisfying nature.

Pastries and Breads:
Mediterranean pastries often lean towards the savory side, with rich, flaky layers and fillings that incorporate the bounty of the region's produce. **Spanakopita** (Greek spinach pie) and **börek** (Turkish pastry filled with cheese or spinach) are popular choices, offering a comforting combination of flaky pastry, savory fillings, and sometimes a hint of spice. **Croissants** and **pain au chocolate** have found their place in Mediterranean breakfast tables as well, especially in France and coastal regions, reflecting the French influence on Mediterranean cuisine. A warm, buttery pastry paired with coffee or fresh juice makes for a leisurely start to the day.

Fresh and Hearty Starts to Your Day: Mediterranean-Inspired Smoothies, Toasts, and More

While traditional Mediterranean breakfasts are often simple, the use of fresh, seasonal ingredients allows for a variety of flavorful, nutrient-packed options. Whether you're looking for a light meal to kickstart your day or a more filling option to fuel your morning, Mediterranean-inspired smoothies, toasts, and bowls are perfect ways to enjoy vibrant and healthy ingredients.

1. **Mediterranean Smoothies**:
    The Mediterranean diet is rich in fruits, vegetables, nuts, and seeds, making it an ideal source of inspiration for delicious and nourishing smoothies. A classic **Mediterranean smoothie** might blend **Greek yogurt** with **citrus fruits** like **oranges** or **lemons**, and a handful of **spinach** or **kale** for an added nutrient boost. You can also incorporate a scoop of **almond butter**, **chia seeds**, or **flaxseeds** for extra protein and healthy fats. For a more tropical twist, try blending **mango**, **coconut**, and a splash of **almond milk** to capture the flavors of the Mediterranean coast.

THE MEDITERRANEAN LIFESTYLE

2. **Avocado Toast with Mediterranean Flair**:
   Avocado toast has become a global breakfast sensation, and the Mediterranean diet offers its own take on this beloved dish. To make a Mediterranean-inspired version, top whole-grain toast with mashed **avocado**, then drizzle with **extra virgin olive oil** and sprinkle with **feta cheese, cherry tomatoes**, and **oregano**. A squeeze of **lemon** adds a refreshing touch, and the result is a nutrient-dense, filling breakfast that brings together the richness of avocado with the fresh flavors of the Mediterranean. For extra protein, you can add a **soft-boiled egg** on top.
3. **Chia Puddings and Breakfast Bowls**:
   Chia seeds, which are packed with omega-3 fatty acids, protein, and fiber, make for an excellent base for a Mediterranean-inspired breakfast bowl. Simply combine **chia seeds** with your favorite **nut milk** (almond, coconut, or oat milk work beautifully) and let it sit overnight in the fridge. In the morning, top it with a variety of fresh fruits like **pomegranate**, **figs**, or **berries**, and sprinkle with a handful of **toasted almonds** or **sunflower seeds**. A drizzle of **honey** or a dash of **cinnamon** will give the bowl a touch of sweetness and spice. This breakfast is not only filling but also packed with nutrients to fuel your day.

THE MEDITERRANEAN LIFESTYLE

Chapter 6:

Appetizers and Small Plates

Meze and Tapas: Mediterranean Snacks to Share

The Mediterranean tradition of **meze** (Greek and Turkish) and **tapas** (Spanish) invites sharing and communal dining, turning food into an experience rather than just a meal. These small, flavorful dishes are designed to be enjoyed with friends and family, fostering conversation and connection.

1. **Meze**:
   In Greece and the Levant, **meze** refers to a spread of small dishes that can range from fresh, vegetable-based dips to grilled meats and seafood. A classic **Greek meze** platter might include a variety of flavors—**tzatziki** (yogurt, cucumber, and garlic dip), **dolma** (stuffed grape leaves), **feta cheese** with **olive oil** and herbs, and **saganaki** (fried cheese). These dishes are meant to be enjoyed together, each bite complementing the others with a balance of freshness, richness, and savoriness. In Turkey, **meze** is similarly varied, with offerings like **hummus, baba ghanoush**, and **kisser** (a bulgur salad with herbs and tomatoes).
2. **Tapas**:
   In Spain, **tapas** serve a similar purpose—small dishes perfect for sharing. From **patatas bravas** (crispy potatoes with spicy tomato sauce) to **gambas al abilo** (garlic shrimp), Spanish tapas are rich in flavor and often feature a mix of fried, grilled, or pickled ingredients. The beauty of tapas lies in the variety—whether served warm or cold, they're a great way to explore a range of textures and flavors. **Chorizo, jamun, olive tapenade**, and **anchovies** are also popular tapas offerings, often paired with a glass of **sherry** or **sangria** for a true Spanish experience.

Classic Dips: Hummus, Tzatziki, and Baba Ghanoush

THE MEDITERRANEAN LIFESTYLE

Dips are a cornerstone of Mediterranean appetizers, and these beloved classics have spread worldwide due to their delicious flavors and versatility. Rich, creamy, and bursting with fresh ingredients, these dips can be paired with bread, fresh vegetables, or crackers.

1. **Hummus**:
   A staple in Levantine cuisine, **hummus** is made from **chickpeas**, **tahini** (sesame paste), **garlic**, **lemon juice**, and **olive oil**. Its silky-smooth texture and nutty flavor make it perfect for dipping, spreading on pita, or topping roasted vegetables. While classic hummus is already a crowd-pleaser, variations such as **red pepper hummus**, **spicy hummus**, or **beetroot hummus** add a unique twist to the traditional recipe.
2. **Tzatziki**:
   Tzatziki is a refreshing Greek yogurt-based dip that combines **cucumber, garlic, dill**, and a touch of **lemon juice**. It's often served as a side dish to grilled meats like **souvlaki** or **gyro**, but it's cool, creamy texture makes it a perfect accompaniment to anything from fresh pita to crudités. The addition of **mint** or **parsley** can provide a bright and herbaceous finish, balancing the richness of the yogurt.
3. **Baba Ghanoush**:
   A smoky, velvety dip, **baba ghanoush** is made from roasted **eggplant**, tahini, garlic, lemon juice, and **olive oil**. The eggplant is charred to bring out its deep, smoky flavor, giving the dip its signature taste. It's often served with warm pita bread and garnished with pomegranate seeds or a drizzle of olive oil, making it both visually stunning and delicious.

Stuffed Delights: Grape Leaves, Pastries, and Pockets

Stuffed foods are a Mediterranean favorite, often highlighting the region's use of fresh herbs, grains, and vegetables, wrapped in delicate pastry or leafy packages. Whether enjoyed as part of a meze platter or as a main dish, these bites are bursting with flavor and textural contrast.

1. **Dolma (Stuffed Grape Leaves)**:
   A quintessential Mediterranean dish, **dolma** are grape leaves stuffed with a mixture of **rice, herbs** (like **dill, parsley,** and **mint**), and sometimes **ground lamb** or **beef**. In Greece, **dolma** is typically served with a side of **tzatziki** or **lemon wedges**, making them the perfect balance of tart, fresh, and savory. In Turkey, the stuffing might include **pine nuts** and **currants**, adding a touch of sweetness to the mix.
2. **Pastries**:
   From **spanakopita** (Greek spinach pie) to **börek** (Turkish pastry), these flaky, savory treats are a Mediterranean staple. Often made with **phyllo dough**, **spanakopita** is filled with a blend of **spinach, feta cheese**, and **herbs**, then baked until golden and crisp.

THE MEDITERRANEAN LIFESTYLE

Börek, a similar pastry popular in Turkey, can be stuffed with a variety of fillings, including **cheese**, **ground meat**, or even **potatoes**.

3. **Stuffed Pockets**:
Mediterranean stuffed pockets come in many forms. From **samosas** in North Africa to **pita sandwiches** in the Middle East, these handheld delights offer a perfect way to enjoy Mediterranean flavors on the go. **Man'oushe** (Lebanese flatbreads) are often stuffed with **za'atar** or **cheese**, while **focaccia** (Italian flatbread) can be stuffed with **rosemary** and **garlic**, offering a soft, savory bite that's perfect for breakfast or a light snack.

---

bulgur wheat salad). These spreads and small bites highlight the Mediterranean's ability to transform humble ingredients into flavorful, satisfying dishes that are perfect for grazing and sharing.

2. **Tapas**:
In Spain, **tapas** are the cornerstone of social dining, allowing people to sample a variety of flavors in one sitting. The tradition of eating tapas is deeply ingrained in Spanish culture, where meals are often spread out over several hours, with friends and family enjoying small plates throughout the evening. Tapas range from simple **olives** and **cheese** to more elaborate dishes like **patatas bravas** (fried potatoes with spicy tomato sauce), **gambas al abilo** (garlic shrimp), and **albondigas** (meatballs in tomato sauce). Tapas allow you to experience the diversity of Spanish ingredients and flavors, from the smokiness of **pimentón** (paprika) to the sweetness of **romesco sauce**. Tapas are often paired with **Spanish wines** or **sangria**, making them an excellent choice for gatherings and casual meals.

Classic Dips: Hummus, Tzatziki, and Baba Ghanoush

Dips are essential to Mediterranean appetizers, providing a simple yet flavorful way to enjoy fresh bread, vegetables, or other accompaniments. Each region has its own variation, often built around local ingredients and flavor preferences. Here are some of the most beloved dips that are a must-try:

1. **Hummus**:
Hummus, a creamy dip made from pureed **chickpeas**, **tahini** (sesame paste), **lemon juice**, and **garlic**, is a staple across the Eastern Mediterranean and Levantine countries. While the basic ingredients remain the same, variations abound, with some versions incorporating roasted **red peppers**, **spices**, or **olive oil** for extra richness. Served with

warm **pita** or fresh **vegetables**, hummus is not only delicious but also packed with plant-based protein and fiber, making it a nutritious snack or appetizer.
2. **Tzatziki**:
   Tzatziki is a refreshing Greek dip made from **yogurt, cucumber, garlic, lemon juice**, and a touch of **dill** or **mint**. The coolness of the cucumber and yogurt balances the sharpness of garlic, creating a dip that is both savory and hydrating. Tzatziki is traditionally served with grilled meats, particularly **lamb**, and is a must-have alongside **gyros** or **souvlaki**. Its fresh, tangy flavor makes it a versatile accompaniment for almost any Mediterranean dish.
3. **Baba Ghanoush**:
   Originating from the Levant, **baba ghanoush** is a smoky, creamy dip made from roasted **eggplant, tahini, lemon juice**, and **garlic**. The key to a perfect baba ghanoush lies in the roasting process—charred eggplant gives the dip its characteristic smoky flavor, which pairs beautifully with the richness of tahini. Often garnished with **pomegranate seeds, parsley**, or a drizzle of **olive oil**, baba ghanoush offers a velvety texture and deep, savory flavor. It's typically served with warm **pita** or crunchy **vegetables**.

Stuffed Delights: Grape Leaves, Pastries, and Pockets

Stuffed dishes are a beloved part of Mediterranean cuisine, with ingredients like rice, meats, and vegetables wrapped in tender, delicate coverings. These bite-sized delights are perfect for appetizers or small plates, offering a satisfying combination of flavors and textures.

1. **Stuffed Grape Leaves (Dolma)**:
   Dolma (or **dolmades**, in Greek) are grape leaves stuffed with a mixture of **rice, herbs, spices**, and sometimes **ground meat** (such as lamb or beef). In Greece, the filling often includes **lemon juice, olive oil**, and **dill**, giving the dish a fresh, tangy flavor. The tender grape leaves are rolled tightly around the filling and steamed to perfection, resulting in a soft, aromatic bite. Dolma can be served warm or cold and is a perfect addition to a meze platter or as an appetizer for any Mediterranean meal.
2. **Pastries**:
   The Mediterranean is home to a wide variety of **savory pastries**. In Greece, **spanakopita** (spinach pie) and **tropia** (cheese pie) are popular choices, made with flaky **phyllo dough** and filled with **spinach, feta cheese**, and aromatic herbs. These pastries are golden and crisp on the outside, with rich, creamy fillings inside. Similarly, in Turkey, **börek** is a beloved pastry, filled with a variety of ingredients such as **spinach, cheese**, or **minced meat**. These pastries are often enjoyed as a snack, appetizer, or light meal, offering a satisfying combination of crunch and creaminess.

3. **Stuffed Pockets**:
   The Mediterranean is no stranger to stuffed breads and pockets, with dishes like **pita**, **monkish** (Lebanese flatbread with za'atar), and **shah** (Lebanese meat pies) being common in various regions. These dishes use simple dough, stuffed with a range of fillings, from **ground lamb** and **pine nuts** to **cheese** and **spinach**. They're easy to prepare, portable, and make for a perfect snack or appetizer to serve at parties, picnics, or casual gatherings.

Chapter 7:

Salads and Sides

Mediterranean Salads: Fresh, Vibrant, and Healthy

In the Mediterranean, salads are not just an accompaniment—they are often the star of the meal. Fresh, vibrant, and bursting with flavor, Mediterranean salads are made with simple, high-quality ingredients, showcasing the region's bountiful produce. These salads are typically made with fresh herbs, ripe vegetables, and a few well-chosen extras, all dressed in **extra virgin olive oil**, **lemon juice**, and sometimes a splash of **vinegar**.

1. **Greek Salad (Horiatiki)**:
   A classic **Greek salad** is a celebration of the region's best ingredients. The combination of **juicy tomatoes, crunchy cucumbers, red onions,** and **green peppers**, topped with a generous block of **feta cheese**, creates a refreshing, bold dish. The addition of **olives, oregano,** and a drizzle of **olive oil** rounds out the flavors, making this salad both satisfying and healthy. It's a perfect example of how Mediterranean salads rely on the simplicity and quality of fresh produce to create incredible flavor.
2. **Tabbouleh**:
   This famous Levantine salad is a light and refreshing blend of **parsley, tomato, onion, mint,** and **bulgur**, dressed in olive oil and lemon juice. While **tabbouleh** may seem simple, the balance of herbs and grains provides a complex, refreshing flavor. The **parsley** is the star of the show, and the fresh citrusy dressing brings everything together in a bright, harmonious way.

THE MEDITERRANEAN LIFESTYLE

3. **Fattoush**:
   Originating from Lebanon, **Fattoush** is a salad that includes crispy **fried pita bread**, tossed with **romaine lettuce, tomatoes, cucumbers**, and **radishes**. What makes this salad special is its zesty dressing, typically made with **pomegranate molasses, lemon juice**, and **olive oil**, which gives the salad a tangy, slightly sweet flavor that contrasts beautifully with the crunchy pita and fresh vegetables.

Roasted Vegetables and Grains: Simple Sides to Complement Any Meal

In Mediterranean cooking, roasted vegetables and grains are essential side dishes that complement main courses while providing a balance of textures and flavors. Roasting is a technique that enhances the natural sweetness of vegetables and creates a crispy, caramelized texture that makes them irresistibly flavorful.

1. **Roasted Vegetables**:
   Mediterranean cuisine takes full advantage of seasonal produce, often roasting **eggplant, zucchini, carrots, sweet potatoes, bell peppers**, and **tomatoes** to create simple, yet incredibly flavorful sides. The vegetables are typically seasoned with **garlic, rosemary, thyme**, and a drizzle of **olive oil** before being roasted at high heat, allowing them to caramelize and develop rich, deep flavors. Roasted vegetables are the perfect accompaniment to grilled meats, pasta dishes, or served over grains.
2. **Couscous and Quinoa**:
   Couscous and **quinoa** are common grains in Mediterranean cooking, often used as a base for side dishes. **Couscous**, made from steamed semolina wheat, is a staple in North African countries like Morocco and Tunisia. It's often served with **tagine**, stews, or roasted vegetables, and can be flavored with **herbs, raisins**, and **spices**. Quinoa, while not native to the Mediterranean, has become a popular choice for a healthy grain, frequently used in **Mediterranean-inspired grain salads**, mixed with **chickpeas, olives, feta**, and **cucumbers**.
3. **Rice Pilaf**:
   Rice pilaf is another side dish that graces many Mediterranean tables. Often cooked with **onions, garlic**, and **spices** like **cumin** and **turmeric**, rice pilaf can be enhanced with **nuts** like **pine nuts** or **almonds** and dried fruits like **apricots** or **raisins**. The combination of flavors and textures makes it a perfect side to grilled meats, seafood, or roasted vegetables.

Breads and Flatbreads: Pita, Focaccia, and Beyond

THE MEDITERRANEAN LIFESTYLE

Bread is a cornerstone of Mediterranean cuisine, serving as both a side dish and a utensil for scooping up dips, spreads, and main courses. Whether it's the famous **pita** from the Middle East, the **focaccia** from Italy, or the **lavash** from Armenia, the variety of Mediterranean breads is as diverse as the cultures that create them.

1. **Pita**:
   Pita bread is a soft, round, flatbread that's a staple in many Mediterranean and Middle Eastern countries. It's especially known for its pocket, which can be filled with a variety of ingredients like **hummus, falafel,** or **grilled meats**. Pita is often served alongside meze platters, dips, or used to scoop up stews and salads.
2. **Focaccia**:
   Originating from Italy, **focaccia** is a delicious, thick, and airy flatbread that's typically seasoned with **rosemary, garlic,** and **olive oil**. It can be served as a side dish, or enjoyed on its own, often as an appetizer. In some regions of Italy, **focaccia** is topped with ingredients like **tomatoes, onions,** or **olives**, making it a versatile bread that can complement any Mediterranean meal.
3. **Lavash**:
   A traditional **Armenian** and **Georgian** flatbread, **lavash** is a thin, soft bread that is baked on the walls of a clay oven. Lavash is often served alongside grilled meats, salads, or dips and can be used to wrap fillings, much like a wrap or tortilla. Its subtle flavor and pliability make it a favorite of many Mediterranean meals.
4. **Ciabatta and Sourdough**:
   In parts of southern Europe, **ciabatta** (Italy) and **sourdough** (Greece, France) are popular choices for bread. Ciabatta, with its crispy crust and soft, airy interior, is perfect for making sandwiches or served alongside pasta and salads. Sourdough, with its tangy flavor, pairs beautifully with Mediterranean olive tapenade or simply dipped in **extra virgin olive oil**.
5. **Tabbouleh**:
   This refreshing Middle Eastern salad is a vibrant mix of finely chopped **parsley, mint, tomatoes,** and **cucumbers**, dressed in **lemon juice** and **olive oil**. The addition of **bulgur** (cracked wheat) gives the salad body, while the herbs provide a fresh, aromatic kick. Tabbouleh is light yet filling, making it the perfect side dish or a light meal on its own. It's also incredibly versatile and can be adapted by adding pomegranate seeds for a touch of sweetness or **green onions** for extra sharpness.
6. **Fattoush**:
   A staple of Lebanese cuisine, **Fattoush** is a crunchy, zesty salad made with **lettuce, tomatoes, cucumbers,** and **radishes**, tossed with fried pieces of **pita bread** and a tangy **sumac dressing**. The **sumac**, with its tart, lemony flavor, is what sets Fattoush apart, while the crispy pita adds an unexpected but delightful texture. This salad combines a variety of flavors and textures, making it a perfect contrast to heavier dishes like grilled meats or stews.

THE MEDITERRANEAN LIFESTYLE

7. **Italian Panzanella**:
   In Italy, **panzanella** is a summer favorite—a rustic, tomato-based salad made with **stale bread**, **tomatoes**, **cucumbers**, and **red onions**, all marinated in a tangy **red wine vinegar** and **olive oil** dressing. The **bread** absorbs the flavors of the vegetables and dressing, creating a moist yet hearty salad that's perfect for using up leftover bread. This dish is quintessentially Mediterranean, demonstrating the region's resourcefulness and love for simple, seasonal ingredients.

Roasted Vegetables and Grains: Simple Sides to Complement Any Meal

Side dishes in the Mediterranean are often as vibrant and flavorful as the main course. Roasting is a key technique that intensifies the natural sweetness of vegetables, while grains like **quinoa**, **farro**, and **couscous** provide satisfying, nutritious bases for many Mediterranean side dishes.

1. **Roasted Vegetables**:
   Mediterranean roasted vegetables often include **eggplant**, **zucchini**, **bell peppers**, and **sweet potatoes**. Tossed in **olive oil**, seasoned with **garlic**, **oregano**, and **rosemary**, and roasted until golden and tender, these vegetables become a rich, flavorful side dish that can be paired with nearly any main course. Roasted vegetables are a perfect complement to grilled meats, seafood, or served as part of a larger meze platter. For extra depth of flavor, drizzle with **balsamic vinegar** or a squeeze of **lemon** just before serving.
2. **Grains**:
   Mediterranean grains are incredibly versatile, offering both texture and nutritional value. **Couscous**, made from semolina wheat, is commonly served alongside stews or as a base for vegetable salads. **Farro**, a nutty, chewy ancient grain, is often tossed with roasted vegetables or used in salads. **Quinoa**, while not traditionally Mediterranean, has become popular for its health benefits and is often used as a substitute for couscous in modern Mediterranean recipes. These grains can be flavored with **herbs**, **spices**, and a drizzle of **olive oil**, making them satisfying sides to complement any meal.

Breads and Flatbreads: Pita, Focaccia, and Beyond

Bread is at the heart of Mediterranean dining. Whether it's **warm pita** served with hummus or **focaccia** baked with **rosemary** and **sea salt**, Mediterranean breads add texture, flavor, and substance to every meal. Bread is often used to scoop up dips, soak up sauces, or simply served alongside a dish to complement the meal.

THE MEDITERRANEAN LIFESTYLE

1. **Pita Bread**:
   Originating from the Middle East, **pita** is a soft, slightly chewy flatbread that puffs up during baking to create a pocket, making it perfect for stuffing with fillings or using as a wrap. Pita is commonly served with **hummus, falafel,** or **grilled meats**. It's also a key component of the Mediterranean tradition of **meze**, used for dipping or scooping up flavorful spreads. Pita can also be toasted and cut into triangles to serve as a crunchy side for dips.

2. **Focaccia**:
   This Italian flatbread is soft and airy with a golden, crisp crust. **Focaccia** is typically topped with **olive oil, rosemary, garlic,** and **sea salt**, though it can be adapted with other toppings like **olives, sun-dried tomatoes**, or **cheese**. Served warm, focaccia is often eaten as an appetizer, snack, or side dish to accompany meals such as **soup, salads,** or **roasted meats**. Its texture and flavor make it a wonderful contrast to the lighter dishes of the Mediterranean.

3. **Ciabatta and Baguette**:
   In Italy and France, **ciabatta** and **baguette** are iconic breads that are commonly enjoyed with **olive oil** and **balsamic vinegar** or served alongside **cheese** and **charcuterie**. The **ciabatta** has a rustic, airy texture, while the **baguette** is long, crusty, and often served in thin slices to complement rich spreads, dips, and pates.

4. **Lavash and Khubz**:
   In regions like Armenia and Morocco, **lavash** (a thin, soft flatbread) and **khubz** (a round, rustic Moroccan bread) are essential to the dining experience. These breads are perfect for scooping up stews, dips, and meats, reflecting the deep culinary traditions of the Mediterranean's eastern edges.

Chapter 8:

Soups and Stews

Hearty Mediterranean Soups: From Greek Avgolemono to Spanish Sopa de Ajo

Soups are an essential part of the Mediterranean culinary landscape, offering warmth, comfort, and nourishment. These dishes often feature seasonal vegetables, legumes, and aromatic herbs, making them as nutritious as they are flavorful. From the light and tangy to the rich and hearty, Mediterranean soups showcase the diversity of the region's culinary traditions.

1. **Avgolemono Soup (Greece):**
   A beloved Greek classic, **avgolemono** is a comforting, creamy soup made with **chicken**, **rice**, and a smooth, velvety egg-lemon sauce. The word "avgolemono" comes from **"ago"** (egg) and **"lemon"** (lemon), which are whisked together and tempered with hot broth to create a silky finish. The soup is bright and tangy thanks to the lemon, with the chicken and rice adding heartiness. It's typically enjoyed during cooler months but is also a popular dish for those feeling under the weather.

2. **Sopa de Ajo (Spain):**
   Sopa de ajo, or **Spanish garlic soup**, is a rustic, flavorful dish from the region of Castilla. Made with an abundance of **garlic, paprika,** and **broth**, the soup is often enriched with **egg** (poached directly in the broth) and served with **crispy bread**. The garlic infuses the soup with a bold, aromatic flavor, while the egg provides richness and creaminess. Sopa de ajo is a perfect example of how simple ingredients can come together to create a deeply satisfying meal.

3. **Lentil Soup (Various Regions):**
   Another Mediterranean favorite is **lentil soup**, which is made in countless variations across the region. In Turkey and Lebanon, **red lentils** are commonly used, combined with **onions, tomatoes,** and **olive oil**. This version is light yet filling, often spiced with **cumin, paprika,** and **lemon juice** to create a comforting, zesty dish. It's the perfect balance of earthiness and brightness, making it ideal for any time of year.

THE MEDITERRANEAN LIFESTYLE

Slow-Cooked Stews: Moroccan Lamb, Tunisian Harira, and More

Slow-cooked stews are a cornerstone of Mediterranean cooking, especially in North Africa, where the use of spices and slow-braising techniques bring out the deep, rich flavors of the ingredients. These stews often involve a variety of meats, vegetables, and legumes, cooked over low heat for hours, allowing the flavors to meld and develop complexity.

1. **Moroccan Lamb Tagine**:
   The **tagine** is both a cooking vessel and a style of dish, a slow-cooked stew typically made with **lamb, chicken,** or **beef**, and often paired with dried fruits like **apricots** or **prunes**. Moroccan lamb tagine is especially famous for its balance of sweet and savory flavors. **Cinnamon, saffron,** and **ginger** combine with the natural sweetness of dried fruits, creating a beautifully spiced sauce. The lamb, tender from hours of slow cooking, absorbs all the aromatic spices, making each bite melt-in-your-mouth delicious. The dish is often served with **couscous** or crusty bread to soak up the flavorful sauce.
2. **Tunisian Harira**:
   A hearty, flavorful soup-stew hybrid, **harira** is a staple in Tunisia, often served during **Ramadan** to break the fast. Made with **lamb** or **beef, chickpeas,** and **lentils**, it's spiced with a mix of **cumin, coriander, cinnamon,** and **turmeric**. Tomatoes add richness and tang, while fresh herbs like **cilantro** and **parsley** provide brightness. Harira is typically thickened with **flour** and **egg**, giving it a velvety, almost stew-like consistency. It's often eaten with dates or **khubz** (a round flatbread) to scoop up the stew.
3. **Italian Beef Stew (Spezza Tino)**:
   In Italy, **separation** refers to a slow-cooked beef stew that's rich, tender, and deeply savory. **Beef** is browned and then simmered in **red wine, tomatoes,** and **broth** until it reaches melt-in-your-mouth tenderness. Carrots, potatoes, and **celery** are often added, absorbing the flavors of the broth. **Rosemary** and **bay leaves** infuse the stew with aromatic depth, while **parmesan** is often grated on top before serving. This rustic dish is often paired with **polenta** or **crusty bread** to soak up the savory sauce.

Sopa de Ajo, or garlic soup, is a rustic Spanish dish, often associated with the region of Castile and León. This hearty, soul-warming soup is made with **garlic, paprika, olive oil,** and **broth**, creating a rich, aromatic base. The garlic gives the soup its deep, pungent flavor, while **smoked paprika** adds a smoky warmth. Typically, **eggs** are poached directly in the broth, creating a velvety texture, and **chorizo** or **ham** can be added for extra richness. Often served with **crusty bread** to soak up the flavorful broth, **soap de ajo** is the perfect antidote to cold weather and is believed to have medicinal properties.

4. **Lentil Soup (Italy)**:
   In Italy, **lentil soup** is a beloved winter dish that varies by region but always provides the same comforting, hearty experience. Made with **lentils, carrots, onions, celery,** and

sometimes **tomatoes**, this soup is flavored with **garlic** and **rosemary**. A drizzle of **olive oil** and a sprinkle of **Parmesan cheese** finishes off the dish. **Lentils** are a staple in Mediterranean cooking, prized for their high protein content and ability to absorb flavors from the ingredients they are cooked with.

Slow-Cooked Stews: Moroccan Lamb, Tunisian Harira, and More

Stews are a central feature of Mediterranean cuisine, especially in North Africa, where slow-cooked dishes are a way to tenderize meats and meld spices and flavors over time. These stews often incorporate a variety of meats, vegetables, and spices, and are perfect for long, leisurely meals. They represent the essence of Mediterranean hospitality—cooked slowly, savored deeply, and shared generously with family and friends.

1. **Moroccan Lamb Tagine**:
   The iconic **tagine** is a Moroccan stew named after the traditional clay pot in which it's cooked. A **lamb tagine** often features tender lamb, slow cooked with a mix of spices such as **cumin, cinnamon, ginger**, and **saffron**, along with vegetables like **carrots, onions**, and **tomatoes**. The key to a successful tagine is the layering of flavors—the spices should never overpower but should work harmoniously with the rich, tender meat. **Dried fruits** like **apricots** or **raisins** are often added for a subtle sweetness, while **almonds** or **sesame seeds** provide crunch. The stew is typically served with **couscous**, which soaks up the flavorful sauce.
2. **Tunisian Harira**:
   Harira is a thick, hearty soup or stew from Tunisia, typically made during Ramadan to break the fast. It features a rich base of **tomatoes, lentils**, and **chickpeas**, flavored with **cilantro, parsley, ginger**, and **cinnamon**. Often, **lamb** or **beef** is added to the mix, along with **noodles** or **rice** to create a satisfying, filling dish. The combination of spices, legumes, and tender meat makes **harira** both flavorful and nourishing, with a slightly spicy kick from **harissa**, a North African chili paste.
3. **French Provençal Beef Stew (Boeuf Provençal)**:
   Boeuf Provençal is a classic French stew from the Provence region, known for its use of fresh, local herbs and ingredients. The stew features **beef**, slow cooked in **red wine**, **garlic, onions**, and a variety of **Provençal herbs** such as **thyme, oregano**, and **bay leaves**. Root vegetables like **carrots** and **potatoes** are often added to round out the dish. The result is a rich, flavorful stew that encapsulates the essence of southern France—comforting, robust, and infused with the flavors of the land.

THE MEDITERRANEAN LIFESTYLE

Chapter 9: Seafood and Fish

Mediterranean Sea Bounty: Grilled Fish, Seafood Paella, and More

The Mediterranean Sea is home to an incredible variety of fish and seafood, and its bounty is at the heart of many iconic dishes. Whether it's a simple **grilled fish**, a complex seafood **paella**, or a fresh **seafood salad**, the Mediterranean way of preparing fish and seafood highlights the natural flavors of the ocean while celebrating regional techniques and ingredients.

1. **Grilled Fish (Various Mediterranean Regions)**:
   Grilled fish is a quintessential Mediterranean dish, celebrated for its simplicity and bold flavors. A whole **sea bass**, **red snapper**, or **branzino** is often marinated with **olive oil, garlic, lemon,** and **fresh herbs** like **rosemary** or **thyme**. The fish is then grilled over open flames, allowing it to absorb a smoky char while remaining moist and tender. Grilled fish is often served with a side of **roasted vegetables** or a light **salad**, making it a satisfying yet light meal. This preparation allows the natural flavors of the fish to shine through, with the herbs and citrus adding depth without overpowering.
2. **Seafood Paella (Spain)**:
   Paella, the famous Spanish dish from the region of **Valencia**, is a celebration of the Mediterranean's seafood bounty. While paella comes in many varieties, the **seafood paella** is particularly beloved for its combination of fresh **shrimp, mussels, clams, calamari,** and **fish,** all cooked with **saffron-infused rice**. The rice absorbs the rich flavors of the broth, creating a flavorful base that perfectly complements the sweetness of the seafood. A sprinkle of **fresh parsley** and a squeeze of **lemon** are added just before serving, bringing a fresh finish to this comforting, celebratory dish.
3. **Bouillabaisse (France)**:
   The **bouillabaisse** is a rich, flavorful French fish stew that originated in the port city of **Marseille**. Traditionally, this dish combines a variety of **local fish, shellfish,** and **crustaceans**, which are simmered in a broth made with **tomatoes, garlic, saffron, olive oil,** and **herbs**. The dish is often served with a side of **rouille** (a garlicky mayonnaise-like sauce) and **crusty bread**, which adds richness and texture to the flavorful soup. Bouillabaisse is more than just a dish; it's a symbol of the Mediterranean's deep connection to the sea and its fresh, local seafood.

Healthy, Flavorful, and Fresh: Mediterranean Fish Dishes You'll Love

THE MEDITERRANEAN LIFESTYLE

The Mediterranean diet is renowned for its health benefits, and fish plays a crucial role in maintaining a heart-healthy, nutrient-rich eating pattern. Whether baked, grilled, or simmered, Mediterranean fish dishes are full of omega-3 fatty acids, lean protein, and antioxidants, offering a flavorful and nutritious way to enjoy the ocean's offerings.

1. **Baked Fish with Herbs (Italy and Greece):**
   A classic Mediterranean dish, **baked fish** is often prepared by stuffing whole fish (like **trout** or **snapper**) with **garlic**, **herbs**, **lemon**, and sometimes **olives** or **tomatoes**. The fish is then baked until the flesh is tender and flakey. This method preserves the moisture of the fish while infusing it with the aromatic flavors of the herbs and citrus. It's a healthy and low-maintenance dish that lets the fish shine.
2. **Grilled Sardines (Greece and Portugal):**
   Sardines are a popular choice in Mediterranean cuisine, particularly in **Greece** and **Portugal**, where they are often grilled whole and served with a squeeze of **lemon** and a drizzle of **olive oil**. Grilled sardines are smoky, savory, and delicious, with a tender texture that pairs perfectly with the freshness of a side salad. Rich in omega-3s and packed with flavor, grilled sardines are a quintessential Mediterranean dish that's both healthy and satisfying.
3. **Mediterranean Fish Tacos (Spain):**
   A modern Mediterranean twist on a classic Mexican dish, **Mediterranean fish tacos** are made by grilling fresh **white fish** like **tilapia** or **halibut**, then serving it in **soft tortillas** with a **cabbage slaw**, **yogurt sauce**, and a squeeze of **lime**. The addition of **cumin** and **paprika** gives the dish a subtle smoky flavor, while the fresh veggies and yogurt provide a cooling balance to the spiced fish. These tacos are an easy, flavorful way to enjoy Mediterranean flavors with a fresh twist.
4. **Tuna Salad with Olive Oil and Lemon (Various Mediterranean Regions):**
   A simple but flavorful dish, **tuna salad** is a Mediterranean classic that highlights the region's love for fresh, local ingredients. Canned **tuna**, preferably in **olive oil**, is combined with **cherry tomatoes**, **red onions**, **olives**, and a handful of fresh herbs. The salad is dressed with a generous drizzle of **olive oil** and **lemon juice**, with a sprinkle of **oregano** to finish. This salad is refreshing and light but packed with flavor, making it a perfect lunch or light dinner option.

with the **olive oil** and **lemon** enhancing its delicate sweetness while the smoky char from the grill adds a subtle depth. In countries like Greece and Turkey, it's common to enjoy grilled fish as part of a larger **meze** spread, where it's served alongside dips like **tzatziki** or **hummus** and accompanied by **pita** or **flatbread**.

5. **Seafood Paella (Spain):**
   Paella, the iconic Spanish dish from the region of **Valencia**, is a celebration of seafood, rice, and saffron. The dish combines a variety of seafood, such as **shrimp**, **mussels**,

clams, and **squid**, along with aromatic **saffron rice** cooked to perfection in a large, shallow pan. The key to a great **seafood paella** is the **Socarras**—the crispy layer of rice that forms at the bottom of the pan. The flavors of the seafood meld with the **saffron, garlic, tomatoes,** and **paprika**, creating a rich and flavorful dish that captures the essence of the Mediterranean coast. While **paella** is traditionally made with a mix of seafood and meat, the seafood version is particularly popular in coastal regions.

6. **Fried Calamari (Italy and Greece):**
A Mediterranean favorite, **fried calamari** is a simple, yet delicious dish often enjoyed as a starter or appetizer. **Squid** is lightly battered and fried until golden and crispy, then served with a wedge of **lemon** and a side of **garlic aioli** or **tomato-based dipping sauce**. The crispy exterior contrasts with the tender, delicate texture of the squid inside, offering a perfect balance of flavors. It's a popular dish in both **Italy** and **Greece**, often enjoyed at seaside tavernas or during festive gatherings.

Healthy, Flavorful, and Fresh: Mediterranean Fish Dishes You'll Love

Mediterranean cuisine is known for its healthy approach to cooking, especially when it comes to **fish**. Rich in **omega-3 fatty acids**, **vitamins**, and **minerals**, fish is often featured in Mediterranean dishes, offering both nutritional benefits and incredible taste. These dishes focus on freshness, flavor, and simplicity, allowing the natural qualities of the fish to shine.

1. **Baked Fish with Vegetables (Italy and Greece):**
Baked fish is a popular Mediterranean dish, especially in **Italy** and **Greece**, where **sea bass** or **branzino** is often used. The fish is seasoned with **olive oil, lemon, garlic,** and **herbs** like **oregano** or **parsley**, then baked alongside a medley of **seasonal vegetables** such as **tomatoes, zucchini,** and **potatoes**. The baking process allows the flavors of the fish to meld with the vegetables, creating a dish that is both light and satisfying. The dish can be served with a side of **quinoa, couscous,** or **rice** for a more substantial meal.
2. **Grilled Octopus (Greece and Turkey):**
Grilled octopus is a Mediterranean delicacy that offers a unique and slightly smoky flavor, balanced with tender, juicy meat. The octopus is often marinated in **olive oil, vinegar, garlic,** and **lemon juice**, then grilled to perfection. It's typically served with a drizzle of **olive oil** and a sprinkle of **oregano** and is often paired with a side of **salad** or **roasted vegetables**. **Grilled octopus** is a dish that brings out the best of Mediterranean flavors, combining the natural sweetness of the octopus with the earthy, herbal notes of the marinade.
3. **Fish Tagine (Morocco):**
A **fish tagine** is a staple of Moroccan cuisine, where fish is stewed with **tomatoes, onions, garlic,** and a blend of **spices** like **cumin, paprika,** and **saffron**. This slow-

THE MEDITERRANEAN LIFESTYLE

cooked dish is typically prepared in a **tagine**, a traditional Moroccan clay pot that helps infuse the fish with the rich, aromatic flavors of the spices and vegetables. Often served with **couscous** or **bread**, fish tagine is a comforting and flavorful dish that highlights the Mediterranean's use of spices to elevate fresh ingredients.

4. **Tuna Salad (Mediterranean Style)**:

   A **Mediterranean-style tuna salad** is a perfect example of how simple, fresh ingredients can come together to create something truly satisfying. **Canned tuna**, often in **olive oil**, is mixed with **cherry tomatoes**, **cucumbers**, **red onions**, and **kalamata olives**, then dressed with **olive oil**, **lemon juice**, and **oregano**. This salad can be served on its own or accompanied by **pita bread** or **mixed greens**. It's a light yet fulfilling meal that's perfect for lunch or a light dinner. Some variations might include **boiled eggs**, **capers**, or **fresh herbs** for added flavor.

THE MEDITERRANEAN LIFESTYLE

Chapter 10:

Poultry and Meat

Chicken, Lamb, and Goat: The Meats of Mediterranean Cuisine

In Mediterranean cuisine, poultry and meat play a significant role, with **chicken**, **lamb**, and **goat** being the most used. These meats are often prepared in ways that highlight the region's rich flavors, using **olive oil**, **garlic**, **herbs**, and **spices** to create dishes that are both satisfying and flavorful. Whether roasted, braised, or grilled, these meats are central to the Mediterranean diet, often paired with vegetables, grains, and legumes to create well-rounded, nourishing meals.

1. **Chicken**:
   Chicken is the most widely consumed poultry in the Mediterranean and is often prepared in simple yet flavorful ways. In countries like **Greece**, **Turkey**, and **Italy**, chicken dishes are often marinated in a mixture of **olive oil**, **garlic**, **lemon**, and fresh herbs such as **oregano** and **rosemary** before being roasted or grilled. The result is tender, juicy chicken with crispy skin and a burst of aromatic flavor. **Chicken souvlaki, grilled chicken with tzatziki**, or a hearty **chicken and lemon soup** are some of the many ways chicken shines in Mediterranean cooking.

2. **Lamb**:
   Lamb holds a special place in Mediterranean cuisine, especially in countries such as **Greece, Turkey, Morocco,** and **Italy**. Known for its rich, gamey flavor, lamb is often paired with bold herbs and spices like **garlic, rosemary, mint,** and **cumin**. **Lamb kebabs** and **lamb souvlaki** are staples in Greece, while **Moroccan lamb tagine** is a slow-cooked stew made with dried fruits and spices. **Roast lamb** is another favorite, often served at festive occasions and accompanied by **potatoes, vegetables,** and **yogurt-based sauces**.

3. **Goat**:
   While less common than chicken or lamb, **goat** is a beloved meat in parts of the Mediterranean, particularly in **Spain, Italy, Greece,** and **North Africa**. Known for its lean, flavorful meat, goat is often used in **stews** and **braises**, where it is slow cooked to tender perfection. **Goat curry** is popular in some Mediterranean coastal regions, and in

Spain, **goat meat** is often cooked in traditional dishes like **cabrito** (roast young goat). The meat's slightly sweet, earthy flavor pairs beautifully with aromatic herbs, **garlic**, and **tomatoes**, making it a favorite in both savory stews and slow-roasted preparations.

Classic Meat Dishes: From Greek Lamb to Spanish Cochineal

The Mediterranean's rich meat traditions are represented by a variety of iconic, time-honored dishes, each with its own unique preparation method and flavor profile. These dishes are often prepared using the region's abundant herbs, spices, and cooking techniques, creating meals that are both hearty and deeply satisfying.

1. **Greek Lamb Kleftiko**:
   A traditional **Greek lamb kleftiko** is a slow-cooked dish where lamb is marinated in olive oil, lemon, garlic, and herbs, then wrapped in parchment paper or foil and slow-cooked until incredibly tender. The name "kleftiko" comes from the Greek word "klephtism," meaning thief, as it's believed that bandits used to cook the meat this way, burying it underground to keep the smell from giving them away. The result is a deeply flavorful dish where the lamb falls off the bone, infused with the bright flavors of lemon and fresh herbs. Served with roasted vegetables or **potatoes**, it's a meal fit for special occasions or a family feast.
2. **Spanish Cochineal (Suckling Pig)**:
   Cochineal asado, or **roast suckling pig**, is a traditional Spanish dish, especially popular in **Segovia**. The piglet is slowly roasted until the skin is golden and crispy, and the meat inside is tender and succulent. The key to **cochineal** is its long cooking time, allowing the fat to render and crisp the skin without drying out the meat. The dish is often served with simple sides like **roasted potatoes** and **green beans**, allowing the rich, savory flavors of the pig to be the star of the meal. It's a beloved celebratory dish in Spain, often enjoyed during holidays and special family gatherings.
3. **Moroccan Tagine with Lamb**:
   A **tagine** is both a traditional Moroccan cooking vessel and a beloved dish that showcases the rich flavors of North African cuisine. **Lamb tagine** is slow cooked with spices like **cumin, coriander, cinnamon**, and **turmeric**, often paired with **prunes, apricots**, or **almonds** to create a perfect balance of savory and sweet. The dish is cooked in a **clay tagine pot**, which traps moisture and allows the meat to become incredibly tender, soaking up the aromatic spices. Served with **couscous** or flatbread, **lamb tagine** is a warming, flavorful dish that is perfect for a cozy dinner or special occasion.

azuki**, and **chicken cacciatore** are just a few of the iconic dishes that showcase the versatility of chicken in Mediterranean cooking. Whether served in a hearty stew, grilled on skewers, or

THE MEDITERRANEAN LIFESTYLE

slow cooked with vegetables, chicken in the Mediterranean is typically prepared with ingredients that enhance its natural flavors without overpowering them.

4. **Lamb**:
   Lamb is another cornerstone of Mediterranean cuisine, particularly in Greece, Turkey, and the Middle East, where it is often roasted, grilled, or stewed. Its rich, tender meat pairs wonderfully with the region's array of fresh herbs, spices, and citrus. In **Greece**, **lamb kleftiko**—a slow-cooked lamb dish wrapped in parchment paper with **garlic**, **lemon**, and **oregano**—is a favorite. In **Morocco**, lamb is used in **tagines**, slow-cooked stews that combine the meat with dried fruits like **apricots** or **prunes**, and spices such as **cinnamon**, **cumin**, and **ginger**. The distinctive, savory flavor of lamb makes it a favorite for holiday meals, celebrations, and gatherings.

5. **Goat**:
   Goat meat is another traditional protein in the Mediterranean diet, particularly in **North African** and **Middle Eastern** cuisines. Known for its slightly stronger flavor compared to lamb, goat is often braised or slow-cooked, allowing the meat to become tender and infused with the flavors of the herbs and spices it is cooked with. In **Moroccan** cuisine, **goat** is used in **mechanic**, a dish where the meat is spit-roasted and served with a side of **flatbread**. In **Greece**, **kleftiko** (another variation) can be made with goat instead of lamb, marinated with garlic, **oregano**, and **olive oil**, before being slow cooked to perfection.

Classic Meat Dishes: From Greek Lamb to Spanish Cochineal

Mediterranean cuisine boasts a variety of rich, flavorful meat dishes that highlight the versatility of poultry, lamb, and goat. These classic dishes have been passed down through generations and reflect the unique cooking traditions of the region.

1. **Greek Lamb**:
   Greek lamb dishes are synonymous with rich, tender, and succulent meat, often paired with bold flavors like **lemon, garlic**, and **oregano**. A quintessential Greek dish is **lamb souvlaki**, where cubes of lamb are marinated in a mixture of olive oil, lemon juice, and herbs, then skewered and grilled. Another classic is **Araki stop four noes**, which involves roasting a whole lamb with **potatoes, lemon**, and herbs until the meat is melt-in-your-mouth tender. Lamb is often served during special occasions and celebrations, and its flavor is perfectly complemented by **tzatziki** and **Greek salad**.

2. **Spanish Cochineal (Suckling Pig)**:
   Cochineal, or **suckling pig**, is one of Spain's most iconic meat dishes, especially in the region of **Segovia**. The pig is traditionally roasted whole in a wood-fired oven, resulting in incredibly tender meat and crispy skin. The dish is typically served with **roasted**

THE MEDITERRANEAN LIFESTYLE

potatoes or **vegetables**, and the meat is so tender that it can be cut with the edge of a plate. This dish is often reserved for special celebrations, making it a symbol of festivity and indulgence. The flavors are simple—salt, olive oil, and sometimes a touch of **garlic** or **rosemary**—allowing the natural sweetness and tenderness of the pig to shine through.

3. **Moroccan Lamb Tagine**:
One of the most famous Moroccan dishes is **lamb tagine**, a slow-cooked stew made with lamb, vegetables, dried fruits, and a rich blend of spices. **Cumin**, **cinnamon**, **ginger**, and **saffron** are some of the signature spices used to flavor the lamb, while **apricots**, **prunes**, or **raisins** lend a subtle sweetness that balances the dish's savory components. **Tagine** is cooked in a traditional earthenware pot of the same name, which helps retain moisture and flavors as the ingredients cook slowly over low heat. This dish is the epitome of Moroccan comfort food, rich, aromatic, and deeply satisfying.

THE MEDITERRANEAN LIFESTYLE

Chapter 11:

Pasta and Grains

Italian Pasta Perfection: Sauces, Shapes, and Simple Dishes

No discussion of Mediterranean cuisine would be complete without **pasta**—arguably the most iconic food of **Italy** and a true symbol of Mediterranean culinary tradition. Pasta is incredibly versatile and can be paired with countless sauces, from rich, meaty ragu to light, fresh tomato-based options. Each region of Italy has its own specialty pastas, shapes, and techniques, but the fundamental idea remains the same: pasta is meant to showcase the flavors of the region, whether through the simple addition of olive oil and garlic or the complex layering of slow-cooked meats and vegetables.

1. **Pasta Shapes**:
   In Italy, pasta is not just about the sauce—it's also about the shape. The shape of the pasta plays a crucial role in how it holds and interacts with the sauce. For example, **spaghetti** is perfect for lighter sauces like **marinara** or **agio e olio** (garlic and oil), while **pappardelle** work wonderfully with heavier, richer sauces like **wild boar ragu**. Shorter pastas like **penne** or **rigatoni** are ideal for thicker sauces, as their ridges and tube shapes help capture the sauce, delivering a hearty bite with every forkful. **Fusilli, farfalle**, and **orecchiette** are popular in different regions of Italy, each contributing its own unique texture to the dish.
2. **Pasta Sauces**:
   The beauty of Italian pasta lies in its simplicity, where the quality of ingredients shines through in each dish. Classic Italian pasta sauces include:
   - **Marinara Sauce**: A fresh, bright tomato sauce made with **San Marzano tomatoes**, garlic, olive oil, and **basil**. It's the essence of **Italian simplicity**, allowing the sweetness of the tomatoes to shine.
   - **Pesto**: Originating from **Genoa** in **Liguria**, **pesto** is made by blending fresh **basil, garlic, pine nuts, parmesan**, and **olive oil** into a fragrant green sauce that pairs perfectly with **trofie** or **ternate**.

- **Bolognese**: A rich, meaty sauce made with **ground beef**, **pork**, or **veal**, **tomatoes**, **onions**, **carrots**, and **celery**, simmered low and slow to develop deep, savory flavors. It's typically paired with **tagliatelle** or **fettuccine**.

Pasta is also a wonderful base for **stuffed pastas** like **ravioli** and **tortellini**, which can be filled with ingredients ranging from **ricotta and spinach** to **meat** or **pumpkin**, all served with complementary sauces or even just a drizzle of melted butter and sage.

Grain-Based Delights: Couscous, Risotto, and Beyond

Grains are an essential part of the Mediterranean diet, offering heartiness, nutrition, and flexibility. In addition to pasta, grains like **couscous**, **risotto**, and **bulgur** form the base for many Mediterranean dishes, absorbing rich flavors and adding a satisfying texture to meals.

1. **Couscous** (North Africa):
   Couscous, a staple of **North African** cuisine, is made from steamed semolina wheat. It's incredibly versatile and is often served as a side dish, main course, or even a dessert (when paired with dried fruits and nuts). The fine grains of couscous absorb the flavors of whatever they are paired with—whether it's a flavorful **tagine** (a slow-cooked stew) or **roasted vegetables**. In countries like **Morocco**, **Algeria**, and **Tunisia**, couscous is often served with lamb, chicken, or seafood, and topped with a mix of dried fruits and nuts for added texture and sweetness.
2. **Risotto** (Italy):
   Risotto is a creamy, comforting dish made from **arborio rice**, a short-grain rice that absorbs liquid beautifully, creating a luscious texture. While it is most associated with **Northern Italy**, risotto is enjoyed throughout the Mediterranean in a variety of forms. **Risotto all Milanese**, flavored with **saffron**, is a classic from Milan, while **seafood risotto** from the coastal regions of **Liguria** and **Venice** highlights fresh fish and shellfish. Risotto can also be made with **vegetables**, **mushrooms**, or **cheese**, offering endless possibilities for different flavors. The key to a perfect risotto lies in the slow, careful stirring and gradual addition of broth to achieve the ideal creamy consistency.
3. **Bulgur Wheat** (Middle East):
   Bulgur wheat, a key ingredient in many **Middle Eastern** dishes, is made from cracked wheat that has been partially cooked, making it quick and easy to prepare. It's used in **tabbouleh**, a refreshing salad, and in hearty dishes like **kibbeh** (a dish made of bulgur and ground meat). Bulgur can also be used as a base for pilafs, paired with vegetables, nuts, and herbs to create a flavorful and nutritious side dish. Its versatility and ability to absorb flavors make bulgur a popular ingredient in Mediterranean kitchens.

like **penne**, **rigatoni**, and **farfalle** are ideal for thicker, chunkier sauces, as their ridges or folds help to trap the sauce. **Orecchiette**, the small, ear-shaped pasta from **Puglia**, is perfect for pairing with robust, vegetable-based sauces like **broccoli rabe** and **sausage**. Each pasta shape is designed to complement certain textures and sauce types, elevating the overall dish.

4. **Classic Pasta Dishes**:
   Some of the most beloved pasta dishes in Italy are incredibly simple, letting the ingredients shine through. **Spaghetti all Carbonara**—a rich and creamy combination of eggs, **pecorino Romano**, **guanciale** (cured pork cheek), and **black pepper**—is a Roman classic. **Pasta al Pomodoro** (pasta with tomato sauce) is another simple yet profound dish, often made with fresh, ripe tomatoes, **garlic**, and a drizzle of **extra virgin olive oil**. In **Sicily**, **pasta all Norma** pairs **rigatoni** with a sauce made from **eggplant**, **tomatoes**, and **ricotta Salata**, embodying the island's abundance of fresh produce. Whether served with seafood, meat, or vegetables, pasta is the heart of Italian cuisine.

Grain-Based Delights: Couscous, Risotto, and Beyond

While pasta may dominate in Italy, other Mediterranean regions showcase the rich variety of grains, turning them into delicious, satisfying dishes that reflect the diversity of the region. From **couscous** in North Africa to **risotto** in Italy and **pilaf** in the Levant, grains are used as a base for both side dishes and hearty mains.

1. **Couscous (North Africa)**:
   Couscous is a staple in many North African countries, including **Morocco**, **Tunisia**, and **Algeria**, where it is often served as a side dish to complement stews, tagines, or grilled meats. **Couscous** is made from **semolina** wheat, steamed until light and fluffy. It's typically served with a stew or sauce, such as the rich, spiced **lamb tagine** or **vegetable stew**. The grains absorb the savory juices from the stew, creating a perfectly balanced dish. In some regions, **couscous** is prepared as a main dish, topped with **roasted vegetables**, **chickpeas**, and **raisins** for a sweet and savory combination.
2. **Risotto (Italy)**:
   Risotto is a classic Italian dish, particularly from the northern regions, and it's all about technique. The key to a perfect **risotto** is in the slow addition of warm **broth** to **arborio rice**, allowing the rice to release its starch and create a creamy, velvety texture. **Risotto all Milanese**, with **saffron**, is one of the most iconic Italian versions, known for its rich, golden color and luxurious flavor. **Seafood risotto**, made with **shrimp**, **mussels**, and **squid**, is a popular choice along Italy's coastlines, while **mushroom risotto** brings the earthy flavors of the forest to the table. Each variation showcases the versatility of this grain-based dish, highlighting seasonal ingredients and regional flavors.

THE MEDITERRANEAN LIFESTYLE

3. **Pilaf (Levant & Eastern Mediterranean)**:
   In the Levant and Eastern Mediterranean, **pilaf** (or **pilaf** in Turkish) is a beloved dish made by simmering **rice** in a flavorful broth, often with **spices** like **cumin**, **cinnamon**, and **cardamom**. **Pilaf** can be served as a side dish or as a main, often accompanied by **chicken**, **lamb**, or **vegetables**. The dish is popular in countries like **Turkey**, **Lebanon**, and **Syria**, where it's served as part of a **meze** spread or with grilled meats. One popular version is **rice pilaf with vermicelli**, where thin strands of pasta are lightly browned before the rice is added, lending a nutty flavor to the dish. The grains absorb the spices and juices, creating a rich and aromatic base that pairs perfectly with the rest of the meal.

4. **Barley and Farro**:
   In regions like **Italy** and the **Mediterranean coast**, **barley** and **farro** are used to make rustic, satisfying dishes. **Farro**, an ancient grain, is often cooked in soups or served as a side dish, often mixed with vegetables, **olive oil**, and **lemon**. It's a hearty, nutty alternative to rice and is a great base for Mediterranean salads. **Barley** is another grain commonly used in **soups** and **stews**, offering a chewy texture and nutty flavor. Both grains are packed with fiber and protein, making them a healthy and filling addition to any Mediterranean table.

Grains in Mediterranean cuisine are more than just fillers; they are key to creating dishes that are both nutritious and delicious. Whether in a bowl of **risotto**, a plate of **couscous**, or a serving of **pilaf**, grains form the foundation for meals that highlight the region's diverse flavors, from the tanginess of lemon to the earthiness of **rosemary** and **garlic**. These dishes are perfect examples of how simple ingredients can come together to create something extraordinary.

creating a dish that is both hearty and comforting. **Lasagna**, another Italian classic, features layers of **pasta**, **meat sauce**, **béchamel**, and **cheese**, baked to perfection. The beauty of Italian pasta lies in its ability to be adapted, with each region contributing its own unique twist based on local ingredients and traditions.

5. **Pasta Sauces**:
   The variety of sauces in Italian cuisine is staggering, each with its own distinct flavors and textures. **Pesto** from **Liguria**—a blend of fresh **basil**, **garlic**, **pine nuts**, **Parmesan**, and **extra virgin olive oil**—is a fresh and fragrant accompaniment to **trofie** or **fettuccine**. **Bolognese**, a slow-cooked meat sauce from **Emilia-Romagna**, is rich and full of depth, typically served with **tagliatelle**. The key to perfect pasta sauce is balance: the right amount of seasoning, the right texture, and the perfect harmony between pasta and sauce.

THE MEDITERRANEAN LIFESTYLE

Grain-Based Delights: Couscous, Risotto, and Beyond

While pasta is the star of Italian cuisine, **grains** like **couscous**, **rice**, and **farro** also play a central role in Mediterranean cooking. These grains are often used in hearty side dishes, salads, and main courses, absorbing the flavors of the seasonings and ingredients they're cooked with.

1. **Couscous**:
   Couscous is a staple in **North African** and **Middle Eastern** cuisines and has found its way into Mediterranean kitchens across the region. Traditionally made from **semolina wheat**, couscous is steamed and can be served as a side dish or incorporated into stews and salads. In Morocco, **couscous** is often paired with **lamb**, **vegetables**, and **spices** like **cumin**, **coriander**, and **cinnamon**. The delicate texture of couscous makes it a perfect vessel for soaking up flavorful broths, and it is often served alongside **tagines**, rich stews, and roasted meats.

2. **Risotto**:
   Risotto, the creamy, comforting rice dish from **Italy**, is a cornerstone of **Northern Italian** cooking. The key to making a perfect risotto is in the technique: the rice is cooked slowly in a flavorful broth, stirring constantly to release the starch and create a creamy, velvety texture. **Risotto all Milanese** is perhaps the most famous version, made with **saffron** to give the rice a beautiful golden hue. Other variations include **mushroom risotto**, **seafood risotto**, and **lemon risotto**, each offering a distinct flavor profile based on the ingredients.

3. **Farro and Other Ancient Grains**:
   Farro, a hearty ancient grain, is a staple in the Mediterranean diet, particularly in Italy. It has a nutty flavor and chewy texture, making it ideal for soups, salads, and side dishes. Farro is often combined with **roasted vegetables**, **fresh herbs**, and a light **lemon dressing** to create a refreshing grain salad. Other ancient grains like **quinoa** and **bulgur** are also popular in Mediterranean cooking, often used to create light, nutrient-dense salads and side dishes.

4. **Barley and Rice**:
   In many Mediterranean cultures, **barley** and **rice** are often used in hearty, filling dishes. **Barley** is often found in **soups** and **stews**, adding texture and heartiness. In Spain, **paella** is traditionally made with **short-grain rice**, which absorbs the rich flavors of saffron, seafood, or meats. In **Greece**, **pilaf** (a rice dish cooked in broth with vegetables, herbs, and sometimes meat) is a common side dish to grilled meats or seafood.

THE MEDITERRANEAN LIFESTYLE

Chapter 12:

Vegetarian and Vegan Mediterranean Dishes

Plant-Based Mediterranean: Flavors that Shine without Meat

The Mediterranean diet is known for its emphasis on fresh, seasonal vegetables, legumes, and grains. While meat and seafood play prominent roles in many dishes, the plant-based offerings are equally rich in flavor, texture, and nutrition. Mediterranean cuisine's emphasis on **olive oil**, **herbs**, **garlic**, and **fresh produce** creates vibrant, satisfying dishes that don't rely on animal products to deliver complex, mouth-watering flavors.

1. **Vegetables at the Heart of Mediterranean Cooking**:
   At the heart of many Mediterranean meals are vegetables that are naturally sweet, savory, and packed with nutrients. The region's warm climate supports a bounty of **tomatoes**, **eggplants, zucchini, peppers**, and **leafy greens** like **spinach, chard**, and **arugula**. These ingredients are often roasted, grilled, or slow-cooked, bringing out their natural sweetness and richness. In **Greece, bream** (a roasted vegetable medley with **olive oil** and **oregano**) is a common side dish, while in **Turkey, imam bailli** (stuffed eggplant) is a beloved vegetarian classic.
2. **Legumes and Grains**:
   The Mediterranean diet places a strong emphasis on **beans, lentils**, and **chickpeas**, which are not only protein-rich but also filling and satisfying. **Hummus**, made from **chickpeas**, **tahini, lemon juice**, and **olive oil**, is a popular spread or dip, while **falafel** (fried chickpea fritters) is a staple in countries like **Lebanon** and **Israel**. **Lentils** form the base of dishes like **lentil soup** in Italy or **mujadara** (lentils with rice and caramelized onions) in Lebanon. **Couscous** and **bulgur** are also key staples in Mediterranean plant-based cuisine, often used in **tabbouleh** or paired with roasted vegetables and herbs.

Healthy, Vibrant Dishes: From Veggie-Loaded Tagine to Stuffed Eggplant

THE MEDITERRANEAN LIFESTYLE

Mediterranean vegetarian dishes are a celebration of color, texture, and taste. Whether slow-cooked, grilled, or served fresh, these dishes are hearty, flavorful, and naturally nutritious. The variety of cooking techniques used—roasting, braising, grilling, and even pickling—ensures that the plant-based ingredients remain interesting and satisfying.

1. **Veggie-Loaded Tagine (Morocco)**:
   The North African **tagine** is a slow-cooked stew traditionally made with lamb or chicken, but it's equally delicious when prepared with seasonal vegetables. A **vegetable tagine** typically includes root vegetables like **carrots, sweet potatoes, parsnips**, and **pumpkin**, combined with **chickpeas, tomatoes**, and **onions**. The vegetables are braised in a blend of **spices** such as **cumin, cinnamon**, and **turmeric**, along with **dried fruit** like **apricots** or **raisins** for added sweetness. The result is a hearty, deeply flavored stew that's perfect served over **couscous** or with flatbread.
2. **Stuffed Eggplant (Imam Bamyili, Turkey)**:
   Imam bailli, or "the imam fainted," is a classic Turkish dish that features **eggplant** stuffed with a fragrant mixture of **onions, tomatoes, garlic**, and **olive oil**. The dish is slow-cooked to allow the eggplant to absorb the flavors of the stuffing while becoming meltingly tender. The dish is served at room temperature and can be enjoyed as part of a meze platter or as a light main course. The richness of the eggplant is balanced by the tangy-sweet tomatoes and aromatic garlic, making it a flavorful and satisfying vegan option.
3. **Chickpea and Spinach Stew (Spain)**:
   In Spain, **chickpeas** are often used in hearty, flavorful stews. One such dish is **garbanzos con Espinas's**—a comforting, savory stew made with **chickpeas** and **spinach**, simmered in a base of **onions, garlic**, and **tomatoes**, and flavored with **paprika**. It's a simple, budget-friendly dish that's packed with fiber, protein, and vitamins. The **smoked paprika** gives it a warm, earthy flavor, while the **spinach** adds freshness and a burst of color.

Mediterranean Vegan Staples and Superfoods

Mediterranean plant-based dishes are not just satisfying but also incredibly nutritious. A Mediterranean vegan diet includes a wealth of **fiber, healthy fats, antioxidants**, and **phytonutrients**. **Olive oil, avocados**, and **nuts** provide healthy fats, while **legumes, whole grains**, and **leafy greens** deliver essential nutrients and protein. The region also boasts a variety of **superfoods** like **pomegranate, figs, olive oil**, and **herbs** such as **oregano, parsley**, and **mint**, which are packed with antioxidants that support overall health.

THE MEDITERRANEAN LIFESTYLE

Mediterranean cuisine provides endless inspiration for those looking to explore vibrant, plant-based dishes. Whether you're a dedicated vegan or simply looking to incorporate more plant-based meals into your diet, these recipes offer a variety of flavors and textures that prove plant-based eating is anything but boring.

in **Turkey**, **imam bailli** (stuffed eggplant with tomato, onion, and garlic) is a beloved dish that showcases how vegetables can be the main event, not just a side dish.

4. **Legumes and Pulses**:
   Legumes, such as **lentils**, **chickpeas**, and **beans**, are staples in Mediterranean vegetarian and vegan cooking. These ingredients are not only a great source of plant-based protein but also add depth and heartiness to dishes. **Hummus**, made from **chickpeas**, **tahini**, **garlic**, and **lemon juice**, is an iconic Mediterranean spread that is both nutritious and versatile. **Lentil soups**, like the **Lebanese lentil soup** with **cumin** and **coriander**, or **falafel**, crispy fritters made from **ground chickpeas** and herbs, are classic examples of how legumes shine in Mediterranean cuisine.

5. **Herbs and Spices**:
   One of the keys to Mediterranean plant-based cooking is the generous use of **fresh herbs** and **spices**, which bring a fragrant and flavorful complexity to the dishes. **Oregano**, **basil**, **parsley**, **cilantro**, **mint**, **cumin**, and **paprika** are just a few of the herbs and spices commonly found in Mediterranean vegetarian recipes. These ingredients are used not only to season food but to build layers of flavor. For example, a **Moroccan chickpea tagine** might feature **cumin**, **cinnamon**, **paprika**, and **turmeric** to create a warm, aromatic dish full of depth.

Healthy, Vibrant Dishes: From Veggie-Loaded Tagine to Stuffed Eggplant

The Mediterranean offers an abundance of plant-based dishes that are vibrant, healthy, and full of life. These dishes not only highlight the beauty of fresh, seasonal vegetables but also offer a perfect balance of textures and flavors, making them satisfy and nourishing without relying on meat or dairy.

1. **Veggie-Loaded Tagine (Morocco)**:
   Tagine, the iconic North African stew, is often prepared with meat, but it also makes an incredible plant-based dish. A **vegetable tagine** can be filled with an array of seasonal vegetables such as **carrots**, **sweet potatoes**, **zucchini**, **eggplant**, and **tomatoes**. It's simmered slowly with aromatic spices like **cumin**, **coriander**, **cinnamon**, and **saffron**, creating a rich and flavorful base. The addition of **dried fruits** like **apricots** or **raisins**

THE MEDITERRANEAN LIFESTYLE

brings a touch of sweetness, while **almonds** or **pistachios** add crunch and texture. This dish can be served with **couscous** or **bread**, making it a filling and balanced meal.

2. **Stuffed Eggplant (Various Mediterranean Regions)**:
   Stuffed eggplant is a quintessential Mediterranean dish that varies by region. In **Greece**, **baked militances** are often filled with a mix of **tomatoes, onions, garlic, olive oil**, and sometimes **rice** or **quinoa** for added texture. In **Lebanon, stuffed eggplant with chickpeas** might be drizzled with a **tahini sauce** for a creamy finish. **Moroccan-style stuffed eggplant** might include **couscous** and **spices**, while **Turkish imam bailli** showcases the beauty of eggplant stuffed with **onions, garlic**, and **tomatoes**, all gently simmered in **olive oil**.

3. **Mediterranean Veggie Mezze**:
   The Mediterranean tradition of **meze** (small plates) offers an array of plant-based dishes that are perfect for sharing. These dishes can include **grilled vegetables, stuffed grape leaves** (dolma) with rice and herbs, **tabbouleh, baba ghanoush** (smoky roasted eggplant dip), and **hummus**. Meze spreads are meant to be enjoyed with fresh **pita bread** or **flatbreads**, making them perfect for gatherings or light meals. These dishes not only offer a variety of flavors and textures but are also packed with nutrients, fiber, and healthy fats.

4. **Mediterranean Salads**:
   A variety of Mediterranean salads can easily be made vegetarian or vegan, offering a fresh, healthy option for any meal. **Fattoush** (a Lebanese salad) is made with fresh vegetables and crispy **pita** bread, while **tabbouleh**, a **Lebanese** herb salad, features **parsley, tomatoes, cucumbers**, and **bulgur wheat**, all dressed with olive oil and **lemon juice**. These salads are naturally vegan, light, and full of flavor. Another refreshing choice is the **Greek village salad**, which combines **tomatoes, cucumbers, red onions**, and **olives**, topped with **feta** (optional for a vegan version) and drizzled with **olive oil** and **oregano**.

Mediterranean vegetarian and vegan dishes reflect the region's commitment to fresh, wholesome ingredients, celebrating the vibrant flavors that can be achieved through simple preparation. By focusing on vegetables, legumes, whole grains, and fresh herbs, the Mediterranean offers an abundance of plant-based meals that are both nourishing and satisfying. Whether you are following a plant-based lifestyle or simply looking to incorporate more vegetables into your diet, these dishes provide a beautiful balance of flavors and textures that will leave you feeling energized and satisfied.

THE MEDITERRANEAN LIFESTYLE

Chapter 13:

Mediterranean Desserts

Sweet Mediterranean Treats: Baklava, Tiramisu, and More

Desserts in the Mediterranean region are often made with simple yet luxurious ingredients such as **honey, nuts, fruit, yogurt,** and **rich pastries**. These treats are not overly sweet but focus on creating depth and balance of flavors using natural sugars and fresh ingredients. Mediterranean desserts are known for their intricate textures and the balance between **crunchy, creamy,** and **flaky** elements. Here are some of the most beloved sweet treats from across the region:

1. **Baklava (Turkey, Greece, Middle East):**
   Baklava is one of the most famous desserts of the Mediterranean, beloved for its delicate, flaky layers of **phyllo dough, butter,** and **honey syrup**. In Turkey and Greece, it is often filled with a mixture of **crushed pistachios, walnuts,** or **hazelnuts**. The sweet, sticky syrup, flavored with **rose water** or **orange blossom water**, soaks into the layers, creating a mouthwatering contrast of crispiness and softness. Baklava is a luxurious dessert often served during special occasions and celebrations.

2. **Tiramisu (Italy):**
   Tiramisu, a classic Italian dessert, is a rich yet light treat made with **ladyfingers** soaked in **espresso** and layered with a creamy mixture of **mascarpone cheese, eggs,** and **sugar**. The dessert is often topped with a dusting of **cocoa powder** and chilled to allow the flavors to meld together. The combination of coffee, cocoa, and cream creates a dessert that is indulgent yet not overwhelmingly sweet. It's one of Italy's most beloved desserts and a perfect end to any meal.

3. **Knafeh (Middle East):**
   Knafeh is a traditional Middle Eastern dessert made with **shredded phyllo dough** or **semolina**, layered with a filling of **sweetened cheese** or **custard**, and then baked until golden. The dessert is then soaked in a **sugar syrup** flavored with **rose water** or **orange blossom water**, giving it a fragrant sweetness. Knafeh is often served warm and topped with **crushed pistachios** for added crunch. It's especially popular in Lebanon, Palestine, and Jordan and is often enjoyed during religious holidays.

THE MEDITERRANEAN LIFESTYLE

Fruit-Based Delights: Sorbets, Cakes, and Pies

In Mediterranean desserts, **fresh fruits** play a starring role, providing natural sweetness and vibrant flavor profiles. Whether in the form of a refreshing **sorbet**, a zesty **fruit pie**, or a light **fruit cake**, Mediterranean chefs use the region's abundant fruits to create light, healthy, and delicious desserts. The use of citrus, stone fruits, and berries is especially prevalent.

1. **Fruit Sorbets (Various Mediterranean Regions):**
   Sorbets are a refreshing way to enjoy fruit, especially during the hot summer months in Mediterranean countries. Made from fresh **fruit purée**, **water**, and **sugar**, sorbets offer an intense fruit flavor without the richness of cream. Citrus-based sorbets, such as **lemon**, **orange**, or **grapefruit**, are particularly popular, providing a tart and refreshing palate cleanser after a meal. In Italy, **limoncello sorbet** made from the famous lemon liqueur from the **Amalfi Coast** is a luxurious treat enjoyed during the warmer months.

2. **Almond Cake (Spain):**
   Almond cake, or **tartar de almendro**, is a popular dessert in Spain and parts of Italy. Made with **ground almonds**, **eggs**, and **sugar**, this cake has a moist, dense texture and is typically flavored with **citrus zest** (like **lemon** or **orange**) and a hint of **almond extract**. It is naturally gluten-free and is often served with a drizzle of **honey** or a dusting of **powdered sugar**. It pairs beautifully with a cup of **coffee** or a glass of **dessert wine**, such as **Pedro Ximénez** or **Vin Santo**.

3. **Fruity Pies and Tarts (France, Italy):**
   Fruit-based pies and tarts are another favorite in Mediterranean desserts, particularly in **France** and **Italy**. **Tarte's aux Fruits** in France often feature a buttery, flaky crust filled with **pastry cream** and topped with a variety of **seasonal fruits** like **berries**, **peaches**, and **apricots**. In **Italy**, **crostata** (fruit tart) is a rustic dessert made with a **short crust pastry** base, filled with a **fruit jam** (typically **apricot** or **cherry**) and sometimes topped with a lattice crust. These desserts are simple yet satisfying, celebrating the natural sweetness and textures of fresh fruit.

4. **Orange Blossom and Fig Cake (Morocco):**
   Orange blossom and fig cake is a traditional Moroccan dessert that combines the rich flavors of **dried figs** with the delicate fragrance of **orange blossom water**. The cake is moist, flavorful, and often served alongside **mint tea** as a light, refreshing end to a meal. The **figs** provide a natural sweetness, while the **orange blossom** adds a floral, aromatic note that makes this cake unique and unforgettable.

soft sweetness. The key to perfect **baklava** lies in achieving the right balance between crisp, golden pastry and the syrup's aromatic sweetness. This iconic treat is often enjoyed with a cup of Turkish coffee or Greek **frappe** (iced coffee), making it a delightful conclusion to a meal.

5. **Tiramisu (Italy)**:
   Tiramisu, meaning "pick me up" in Italian, is one of Italy's most beloved desserts. This indulgent, no-bake treat layers **Savoyard biscuits** (ladyfingers) soaked in **coffee** or **espresso** with a rich **mascarpone cheese** mixture, and is often flavored with a hint of **cocoa powder** or **coffee liqueur**. Its luxurious, creamy texture combined with the bold, coffee-infused sponge creates a delightful contrast. **Tiramisu** is often chilled for several hours, allowing the flavors to meld and intensify, resulting in a dessert that is both light and decadent.

6. **Kadaifi (Greece, Turkey)**:
   Kadaifi is a Turkish and Greek pastry that is similar to **baklava** but made with finely shredded phyllo dough, which forms a nest-like texture when baked. It's typically filled with **nuts** and drenched in sweet **syrup**, giving it a delightful contrast between crispy edges and a tender interior. The shredded dough allows for more crunch and creates a beautiful, intricate look, making **kadaifi** not only a delicious but also visually striking dessert.

Fruit-Based Delights: Sorbets, Cakes, and Pies

The Mediterranean's abundance of fresh, seasonal fruit makes it the perfect base for light, refreshing desserts. **Citrus, berries, stone fruits**, and **figs** are commonly used in sweet treats, often paired with nuts or yogurt to create flavorful, textural contrasts. These desserts are typically not overly rich but instead focus on bright, natural flavors that celebrate the fruits of the region.

1. **Sorbets and Granitas**:
   Sorbets and **granitas** are icy, refreshing desserts that highlight the Mediterranean's abundant citrus and fruit harvest. Made with pureed fruit, water, and sugar, these desserts are perfect for hot summer days. **Lemon sorbet** is a classic, with its tart, citrusy flavor acting as a palate cleanser after a rich meal. In **Italy, granita di Limone** is a popular Sicilian treat, a shaved ice dessert flavored with **lemons**, offering a cool, tangy, and lightly sweet finish. Other fruit variations, such as **strawberry** or **pomegranate sorbet**, also make for vibrant and refreshing alternatives.

2. **Fruit-Based Cakes and Pies**:
   The Mediterranean also has a tradition of baking **fruit cakes** and **pies** that showcase seasonal produce. **Torta Della Nonna**, a Tuscan classic, is a custard-filled **pie** with a buttery, **short crust** base, often topped with **pine nuts** and **powdered sugar**. In **Spain, tartar de Santiago** is a cake made with **almonds, sugar**, and **eggs**, often served with a dusting of powdered sugar in the shape of the **St. James Cross**. **Fig cakes** are also popular in the Mediterranean, particularly in countries like **Greece** and **Morocco**, where figs are abundant and can be used to create a moist, slightly spicy dessert.

THE MEDITERRANEAN LIFESTYLE

3. **Orange and Almond Cake (Spain, Italy)**:
   Orange and almond cake is a staple in many Mediterranean countries, particularly **Spain** and **Italy**, where citrus fruits are abundant. This moist, fragrant cake combines **almond flour** with **fresh orange juice** and **zest**, creating a delicate, naturally gluten-free dessert. The almonds lend a subtle richness, while the oranges provide a bright, citrusy contrast. In **Spain**, the cake is often served with a light **syrup** or **whipped cream**, making it a perfect treat for any occasion.

Mediterranean desserts are a celebration of the region's natural bounty—**fruits**, **nuts**, **honey**, and **dairy**—combined in ways that highlight their inherent sweetness and richness. Whether it's a nut-filled pastry like **baklava**, a rich Italian **tiramisu**, or a refreshing citrus sorbet, these desserts not only satisfy the sweet tooth but also provide a taste of the Mediterranean's diverse culinary traditions.

THE MEDITERRANEAN LIFESTYLE

Chapter 14:

Drinks and Beverages

Mediterranean Wines and Spirits: Pairing the Best Wines with Mediterranean Flavors

Wine and spirits are integral to Mediterranean culture, with centuries-old traditions that highlight the art of pairing drinks with food. From the **sun-drenched vineyards of Spain** to the **mountainous terroirs of Italy** and **France**, Mediterranean wines are made from some of the world's most revered grape varieties. These wines are often full of character, influenced by the region's rich history, diverse landscapes, and local climate. Alongside wines, the Mediterranean boasts a variety of traditional spirits and liqueurs that pair beautifully with its cuisine.

1. **Mediterranean Wines**:
   The Mediterranean is home to some of the most famous wine regions in the world, each producing wines that perfectly complement the local flavors. In **France**, particularly the **Provence** region, **rosé** wines are light, crisp, and full of citrusy freshness, making them a perfect match for **seafood dishes** and **salads**. In **Italy**, the wines range from the bright, fruity **Pinot Grigio** to the full-bodied **Chianti** and **Barolo**. A glass of **Chianti** is a natural companion to classic **Italian pasta** dishes, especially those with **tomato-based sauces** or **grilled meats**. In **Spain**, **Rioja** and **Tempranillo** are popular reds, rich in fruit and spices, ideal for pairing with **grilled meats** and **paella**. Sancerre from the **Loire Valley** in **France** is a fantastic **white wine** that pairs wonderfully with **Mediterranean fish** and **fresh salads**.

2. **Traditional Mediterranean Spirits**:
   The Mediterranean region is also famous for its **spirits**, often consumed as a digestif after meals or enjoyed during social gatherings. **Ouzo** from Greece is a popular anise-flavored spirit that pairs perfectly with seafood, while **raki** in Turkey offers a similar experience. In **Italy**, **limoncello**, made from fresh **lemons**, is a refreshing post-dinner drink that complements the citrusy flavors in Mediterranean cuisine. **Pastis**, a French anise-flavored spirit, is enjoyed in the South of France and pairs beautifully with a variety of appetizers, such as **olives** and **cheese**.

THE MEDITERRANEAN LIFESTYLE

Refreshing Drinks: Lemonades, Herbal Teas, and Coffee

In addition to wine and spirits, the Mediterranean is home to a wide range of refreshing drinks that are enjoyed throughout the day. From **cool lemonades** to **herbal teas** and **coffee**, these beverages are the perfect way to hydrate and relax while enjoying the sunny, relaxed atmosphere of the Mediterranean lifestyle.

1. **Lemonades and Citrus-Based Drinks**:
   The Mediterranean climate is ideal for **citrus fruits**, and many refreshing drinks are made from freshly squeezed lemons, oranges, or grapefruits. **Lemonade**, often made with **fresh lemon juice**, **sugar**, and **water**, is a simple but refreshing drink enjoyed throughout the region, particularly in the summer months. **Italian lemonade**, known as **limonite**, is typically more tart and tangy, sometimes made with a splash of **sparkling water** for added fizz. In **Spain**, **Naranja** (orange) juice is commonly enjoyed fresh, often squeezed directly from local oranges. In **Morocco**, **mint tea**, made with fresh **mint leaves** and **green tea**, is a popular, refreshing beverage served throughout the day.
2. **Herbal Teas**:
   The Mediterranean's use of **herbs** extends to its many fragrant and soothing **herbal teas**. **Mint tea** is a staple in **Morocco** and other North African countries, where it is often prepared with **green tea** and a generous amount of **fresh mint**. In **Turkey**, **apple tea** is commonly served to guests as a sign of hospitality. **Chamomile tea** is another popular choice across the region, known for its calming properties and ability to aid digestion. **Thyme** and **sage** teas are also enjoyed, often used as remedies for colds or as a soothing drink before bed.
3. **Mediterranean Coffee**:
   Coffee culture in the Mediterranean is both rich and deeply ingrained in daily life. The famous **Turkish coffee** is brewed in a special pot called a **cezve**, often over an open flame, and served in small cups with the grounds left at the bottom. It's a strong, unfiltered coffee that's typically accompanied by a glass of water and sometimes **Turkish delight**. In **Italy, espresso** is the coffee of choice, and it's commonly enjoyed throughout the day, often accompanied by a small pastry. **Greek coffee** is like Turkish coffee, but slightly thicker and sometimes served with a glass of cold water on the side. In **Spain**, **café con leche** (coffee with milk) is popular, especially in the mornings, and is typically paired with a light **pastry** or **toast**.

Barolo—ideal for pairing with **hearty meat dishes** or **aged cheeses**. **Spain** offers rich, bold reds like **Tempranillo** from **Rioja** and **Ribera del Duero**, which are perfect with **grilled meats** and **Spanish tapas**. In **Greece**, you'll find wines like **Assyrtiko** from **Santorini**, known for its crisp

THE MEDITERRANEAN LIFESTYLE

minerality that pairs wonderfully with **grilled fish** and **vegetarian dishes**, or **Xinomavro**, which is robust and earthy, ideal for rich, slow-cooked meats like **lamb**.

2. **Pairing Wine with Mediterranean Dishes**:
   The key to pairing wine with Mediterranean food is to match the **intensity** of the flavors. Light, crisp wines like **Alberino** (from **Spain**) or **Verdicchio** (from **Italy**) work beautifully with seafood dishes and fresh **salads**. Heavier, full-bodied wines such as **Zinfandel** or **Syrah** are excellent companions for grilled meats, **lamb**, or slow-cooked stews like **tagine**. Sweet wines like **Vin Santo** from **Tuscany** or **Muscat** from **Greece** are perfect to accompany rich, **honeyed desserts** like **baklava** or **cannoli**.

3. **Mediterranean Spirits and Liqueurs**:
   The Mediterranean is also known for its diverse range of **spirits** and **liqueurs**, each with distinct regional flavors. **Ouzo** (Greece), an **anise-flavored** spirit, is often served as an aperitif or with **meze**. Similarly, **Rake** (Turkey) is a traditional drink made from **grapes** and flavored with **anise**, typically enjoyed with **fish** or **cheese**. **Pastis**, a popular drink in **Southern France**, is also **anise-based** and often consumed as a refreshing apéritif. For something sweeter, **Limoncello** (Italy) is a tangy, lemon-infused liqueur that pairs perfectly with lighter, **fruit-based desserts** or enjoyed as an after-dinner drink.

Refreshing Drinks: Lemonades, Herbal Teas, and Coffee

Beyond alcoholic beverages, the Mediterranean offers a variety of refreshing, non-alcoholic drinks that perfectly complement the region's warm climate and fresh ingredients. These drinks are not only delicious but also often deeply rooted in tradition, offering a taste of the local culture and a refreshing reprieve from the heat.

1. **Lemonades and Fruit Juices**:
   The Mediterranean is blessed with abundant citrus fruits, and **freshly squeezed lemonade** is a popular drink across the region. In **Italy, limonite** is made with freshly squeezed **lemons, sugar**, and **water**—a simple yet perfect drink to cool off on a hot day. In **Spain, Ghanizada** is a refreshing, slushy version of lemonade made with crushed ice and lemon juice, often sweetened with **cane sugar. Pomegranate juice**, particularly in countries like **Turkey** and **Morocco**, is also a favorite, known for its tart, tangy taste and health benefits.

2. **Herbal Teas**:
   The Mediterranean's love for **herbal teas** is reflected in a wide array of refreshing and calming drinks. In **Morocco, mint tea** is a cherished tradition, prepared with **green tea, fresh mint**, and **sugar**. It's often enjoyed in social settings, with multiple refills offered to guests. **Turkish tea** is another example, often served in small, tulip-shaped glasses,

THE MEDITERRANEAN LIFESTYLE

with a sweet, rich flavor. **Chamomile**, **thyme**, and **sage** teas are common in countries like **Greece** and **Italy**, where herbs are often grown locally and used for both culinary and medicinal purposes.

3. **Mediterranean Coffee**:
Coffee culture in the Mediterranean is rich and varied, with each country offering its unique style of brewing. In **Turkey** and **Greece**, **Turkish coffee** is brewed with finely ground coffee, **water**, and **sugar** in a traditional **cezve** (a small pot), then served in small cups. The coffee is thick, strong, and often accompanied by a glass of water or **Turkish delight**. In **Italy**, espresso reigns supreme, whether enjoyed as a quick shot in a bustling café or sipped slowly after a meal. **Caffè latte**, **cappuccino**, and **macchiato** are also popular choices in Italy, each with its own cultural significance and drinking ritual. **Spanish café con leche** and **French café au lait** are also beloved throughout the region, often served with **pastries** or **croissants** for breakfast.

4. **Iced Coffees and Refreshers**:
During the hot summer months, iced coffee drinks become a staple across Mediterranean countries. The **Greek frappé**, a frothy iced coffee made with instant coffee, sugar, and water, is a quintessential summertime drink. In **Italy, iced coffee** or **granita di caffè** is another popular way to enjoy coffee, where the drink is frozen into ice crystals and served as a refreshing slush. For those looking for a lighter refreshment, **iced herbal infusions**, such as **mint** or **chamomile**, are also common, offering a cooling, caffeine-free alternative.

With these drinks, the Mediterranean lifestyle extends beyond food—it becomes a celebration of moments, flavors, and traditions that have been cherished for centuries. Whether sipping a glass of **local wine**, enjoying a **strong espresso**, or relaxing with a cup of **mint tea**, the drinks of the Mediterranean are as much a part of the culinary experience as the meals themselves.

THE MEDITERRANEAN LIFESTYLE

Chapter 15:

Entertaining Mediterranean Style

Mediterranean Feasts: How to Host a Perfect Dinner Party

Entertaining in the Mediterranean is all about sharing food, celebrating the joys of community, and creating a welcoming atmosphere. Meals are often long and leisurely, with multiple courses served family-style, allowing guests to try a little bit of everything. The Mediterranean way of entertaining emphasizes **generosity**, **hospitality**, and **simple, yet exquisite flavors**. Here's how to host a perfect Mediterranean dinner party that feels like an authentic celebration of the region's culinary traditions.

1. **Creating a Feast**:
A typical Mediterranean dinner party isn't just about the food—it's about the experience. The table should be filled with a variety of **meze** (small plates), which allow guests to sample a range of dishes. Begin with a selection of **dips** like **hummus, tzatziki,** and **baba ghanoush**, served with **pita** or **crusty bread**. Add **olives, cheeses** (like **feta** or **Manchego**), and **stuffed grape leaves**. For the main course, serve larger platters of **grilled meats** like **lamb kebabs** or **chicken souvlaki**, alongside **roasted vegetables** or **grain-based dishes** like **couscous** or **risotto**.

   Mediterranean feasts often have a **paella**, a **tagine**, or **pasta** as a centerpiece—dishes that can feed a crowd and are filled with bold flavors. Finally, end with sweet treats like **baklava, tiramisu,** or a **fruit platter** topped with honey and yogurt.

   The key is to **share**—serve family-style, where guests can help themselves to whatever they like, encouraging conversation and creating an intimate, communal atmosphere.

2. **Course Structure**:
A traditional Mediterranean meal is structured around several courses. You can start with **aperitifs** like **ouzo** or **vermouth**, served with small nibbles. Follow this with a **meze** platter, filled with various appetizers, before moving onto a hearty **main course** that showcases the best of the region's meats, seafood, or grains. End the meal with **desserts**

THE MEDITERRANEAN LIFESTYLE

like **baklava**, **fruit-based tarts**, or **Greek yogurt** drizzled with honey and topped with crushed pistachios. Throughout the meal, offer a selection of wines, **ouzo**, or **raki**, depending on your regional preference.

Creating the Right Atmosphere: Table Settings and Ambiance

The Mediterranean way of entertaining is all about creating a relaxed, comfortable, and inviting environment. The atmosphere should feel like a celebration, with warm colors, simple yet elegant table settings, and an emphasis on communal dining. Here's how to create the right ambiance for your Mediterranean dinner party:

1. **Table Settings**:
   The table should reflect the casual elegance of Mediterranean dining. Use simple, rustic **ceramic plates** and **wooden utensils** for a relaxed vibe, or go for slightly more formal, yet still earthy, settings with **stoneware** or **porcelain** plates and **glassware**. Consider using **linen napkins** and a **natural tablecloth** to create a soft, inviting atmosphere. **Candles** or **tea lights** placed on the table or around the room will add warmth and a touch of romance. In Mediterranean culture, meals are meant to be enjoyed leisurely, so don't rush the dining experience—create a setting that encourages conversation and lingering at the table.

2. **Decor**:
   For the decor, keep it light and natural, with a focus on **fresh flowers**, **herbs**, or **fruit bowls** as centerpieces. **Olives**, **grapes**, **figs**, and **lemons** are all iconic Mediterranean symbols and can make for beautiful, edible centerpieces. Incorporate elements of **wood**, **terracotta**, and **woven baskets** to bring warmth and texture to the dining area. To enhance the Mediterranean feel, use vibrant colors such as **deep blues** and **sunset oranges**, reminiscent of the Mediterranean coast.

3. **Lighting and Music**:
   Lighting is key to creating the perfect atmosphere. In Mediterranean dining, lighting is soft and warm, evoking the glow of a sunset. Use **candles**, **string lights**, or **lanterns** to create a cozy, intimate setting. As for music, play **soft Mediterranean jazz**, **traditional Greek**, or **Spanish guitar music** in the background to set the tone without overpowering conversation. The goal is to create a relaxed, festive ambiance that encourages people to unwind and savor the moment.

4. **The Mediterranean Spirit**:
   The Mediterranean way of entertaining is all about slowing down and enjoying the moment. Don't worry about perfection—focus on the joy of sharing good food with loved ones. As your guests savor the dishes you've prepared, take the time to enjoy the **flavors**, the **conversation**, and the **company**. Whether you're dining indoors or outdoors,

make the experience feel special by celebrating the Mediterranean values of **community**, **hospitality**, and **simplicity**.

course, serve hearty, flavorful dishes like **lamb kebabs**, **grilled fish**, or a **vegetable tagine**. A Mediterranean feast often includes a combination of **grains**, **vegetables**, and **meats**, all seasoned with fresh herbs, citrus, and **olive oil**. **Pasta dishes**, like a simple **spaghetti agio e olio**, or a **paella**, filled with fresh seafood, can also be crowd-pleasers.

For dessert, end the meal with sweet treats like **baklava**, **tiramisu**, or **fruit sorbet**, paired with a rich **Greek yogurt** drizzled with **honey**. **Sliced fruits** like **oranges**, **pomegranates**, and **figs** can be a refreshing and light way to finish off the meal. Throughout the meal, be sure to have plenty of **wine** and **water** on hand to keep guests hydrated, as well as **herbal teas** or **coffee** for a satisfying conclusion.

2. **Serving Family-Style**:
    The key to a Mediterranean-style dinner party is **serving food family-style**, allowing guests to pass dishes around and create their own plates. This encourages conversation and sharing, turning the meal into an event. Large platters of **grilled meats**, **vegetable stews**, or **pasta** are typically placed in the center of the table, with everyone helping themselves. This creates an atmosphere of warmth and connection, where everyone feels included. Don't worry too much about portion control—Mediterranean dining is about abundance and generosity.

Creating the Right Atmosphere: Table Settings and Ambiance

The atmosphere is as important as the food when it comes to hosting a Mediterranean dinner party. The setting should evoke a sense of warmth, relaxation, and effortless beauty. Mediterranean dining takes place in a **casual**, **inviting** environment, where friends and family can gather to enjoy food and conversation.

1. **Table Settings**:
    A Mediterranean table should feel inviting and elegant without being overly formal. Use **simple, rustic tableware**, like **ceramic plates**, **wooden bowls**, and **linen napkins**. **White tablecloths** or **natural linen runners** can add a touch of sophistication while maintaining a relaxed vibe.

    Glassware should be simple yet elegant—**wine glasses** for reds, whites, and rosés, and **water glasses** for guests to stay hydrated. Serve **sparkling water** or **homemade lemonade** in **pitchers** for an authentic touch. To create a sense of celebration, include a few **candles** or **string lights** on the table to add warmth, especially if your dinner party stretches into the evening.

2. **Lighting**:
   The lighting at a Mediterranean dinner should feel soft and welcoming. During the evening, **candlelight** is ideal to create a relaxed, intimate atmosphere. **Lanterns**, **tea lights**, or **hurricane lamps** can be used to add warmth to the setting. If you're dining outdoors, **fairy lights** or a **fire pit** can set the mood and bring an extra layer of charm to your gathering.
3. **Ambiance**:
   Music is another essential element of Mediterranean entertaining. Create a playlist that features **soft, traditional Mediterranean music**, whether it's **Greek bouzouki**, **Italian mandolin**, or **Spanish flamenco**. Keep the music at a volume that encourages conversation without overpowering it. The overall ambiance should feel **unhurried** and **joyous**, where guests can relax, enjoy the flavors, and savor the company around them.

Mediterranean entertaining is about more than just food—it's about creating an experience that engages all the senses. By focusing on generosity, hospitality, and a laid-back atmosphere, you can host a dinner party that brings the flavors of the Mediterranean to life and leaves your guests feeling both nourished and connected.

Chapter 16: The Mediterranean Diet in Everyday Life

Meal Planning for the Mediterranean Diet: Simple Steps for Success

Adopting the **Mediterranean diet** is not just about occasional indulgence in flavorful dishes—it's about making these healthy, vibrant meals a part of your daily routine. The Mediterranean lifestyle emphasizes fresh, seasonal ingredients, balanced meals, and a focus on plant-based foods, with lean proteins and healthy fats. Meal planning is key to staying on track, reducing stress, and making sure you always have delicious, nutritious options available.

1. **Focus on Fresh, Seasonal Ingredients**:
   The foundation of the Mediterranean diet is built on **fruits, vegetables, whole grains, legumes, nuts, and seeds**. Start by shopping seasonally—this will not only ensure that your meals are at their freshest, but also keep things interesting. Each season brings its own unique selection of produce, so there's always something new to explore. For

example, **summer** might mean **tomatoes**, **zucchini**, and **berries**, while **fall** might bring **squash**, **root vegetables**, and **apples**.

2. **Incorporate Healthy Fats**:
   The **Mediterranean diet** is known for its use of **olive oil** as the primary fat source, which is rich in heart-healthy **monounsaturated fats**. Stock your pantry with high-quality **extra virgin olive oil** for cooking, dressing salads, and drizzling over roasted vegetables. **Nuts** like **almonds** and **walnuts**, and **seeds** like **chia** and **flaxseed**, can be sprinkled on salads or added to smoothies for extra crunch and nutrition.

3. **Plan Balanced Meals**:
   A balanced Mediterranean meal typically includes a variety of **vegetables**, a **lean protein** (like **fish**, **chicken**, or **legumes**), a whole grain, and a healthy fat. Planning meals around these core components ensures that you get a range of nutrients. For example, a typical dinner might be **grilled salmon** with a **quinoa salad** filled with **tomatoes**, **cucumbers**, and **olive oil**, plus a side of **steamed broccoli**. Breakfast could include **Greek yogurt** with **berries**, **walnuts**, and a drizzle of **honey**. Keep your meals simple, but always varied—this way, you're always excited for your next meal.

Cooking for One, Two, or a Family: Adapting Mediterranean Meals for Every Need

Whether you're cooking for yourself, a partner, or a family, the Mediterranean diet offers flexibility to adapt meals to suit different needs and tastes. Here are some tips for portioning, preparing, and adapting your Mediterranean-inspired meals for every situation.

1. **Cooking for One**:
   Cooking for one doesn't have to be complicated or time-consuming. Many Mediterranean dishes can easily be scaled down. For example, prepare a single **grilled chicken breast** with a side of **roasted vegetables** and a **small salad** dressed with **olive oil** and **lemon juice**. You can also make a **grain bowl** with **quinoa** or **farro**, topped with **hummus**, **avocado**, and some **cherry tomatoes**. Leftovers can be stored for a quick lunch the next day or repurposed into a new dish. A leftover chicken breast can be added to a **Mediterranean wrap** with **tahini sauce** or diced and tossed into a **grain-based salad**.

2. **Cooking for Two**:
   When cooking for two, you can prepare slightly larger portions and share. A great option is to make a **Mediterranean-style pasta**, like **spaghetti agio e olio** with **shrimp** and **spinach**, or a **vegetable tagine** that can be served with **couscous**. A large **Greek salad** with **feta**, **olives**, **cucumbers**, and **tomatoes** makes a perfect side dish that can be enjoyed by both. **Rice dishes**, such as **risotto** or **pilaf**, can be easily doubled to feed two people.

THE MEDITERRANEAN LIFESTYLE

3. **Cooking for a Family**:
   Cooking for a family offers the opportunity to create bigger, shareable meals. **Family-style** dishes like **paella**, **roast chicken**, or a **large vegetable stew** are perfect for feeding multiple people. You can prep **meatballs** (like **lamb** or **chicken**) or make a big batch of **falafel** to serve with pita bread and a variety of **dips**. For a more balanced meal, include a variety of sides such as **roasted vegetables, whole grain salads**, and **simple green salads**. Since Mediterranean food often gets better with time, these family meals are great for leftovers, making it easier to plan for the week ahead.

2. **Stock Your Pantry with Mediterranean Essentials**:
   To simplify meal planning, keep your pantry stocked with key Mediterranean staples. **Olive oil, garlic, canned tomatoes, chickpeas, lentils,** and **whole grains** like **quinoa, bulgur,** and **brown rice** are staples that can be used in a wide variety of dishes. You'll also want to have **herbs** like **oregano, basil, thyme,** and **rosemary**, as well as spices like **paprika** and **cumin** to add flavor without added salt. **Cheeses** such as **feta, parmesan,** and **pecorino** are perfect for grating over salads, pasta, and grain bowls, while **Greek yogurt** and **hummus** are great snacks or accompaniments.

3. **Meal Prep and Batch Cooking**:
   Meal prepping can help you save time during the week and ensure that you have healthy meals ready to go. Consider making a big batch of **vegetable soup, grilled chicken,** or **quinoa salad** at the start of the week. These dishes can be easily repurposed for different meals: for example, grilled chicken can be served with **salads, wraps,** or **whole grains**. By cooking in batches, you can mix and match meals throughout the week while reducing the time spent in the kitchen.

4. **Simple Meal Structure**:
   A typical Mediterranean meal is often built around a few key elements: a variety of **vegetables, whole grains, healthy fats** like **olive oil**, and **lean proteins** (fish, chicken, legumes). For example, a meal might include a **grain salad** with **chickpeas, tomatoes, cucumbers, olives,** and a light dressing of **olive oil** and **lemon**, alongside a piece of **grilled fish**. By focusing on simple components that can be prepared in advance and combined in different ways, meal planning becomes both efficient and exciting.

Cooking for One, Two, or a Family: Adapting Mediterranean Meals for Every Need

Whether you're cooking for yourself, a partner, or your whole family, the beauty of Mediterranean cooking lies in its flexibility. Many dishes can be easily scaled up or down, making it perfect for any household size. Here's how to adapt Mediterranean meals to suit different needs:

THE MEDITERRANEAN LIFESTYLE

1. **Cooking for One**:
   If you're cooking solo, **Mediterranean meals** are often quick, easy, and don't require a lot of prep time. opt for **grain bowls, salads,** or **vegetable stir-fries** that use whatever you have on hand. A simple **tomato and mozzarella salad** with fresh **basil** and a drizzle of **balsamic vinegar** can be a satisfying meal. For proteins, keep portions small but flavorful—grilled **chicken breasts** or a piece of **salmon** can be served with a side of **roasted vegetables** or a small **quinoa** salad. The Mediterranean diet encourages meals that don't have to be complicated, allowing you to eat well without spending a lot of time in the kitchen.

2. **Cooking for Two**:
   When cooking for two, you can make larger portions of your favorite dishes, like **pasta with pesto, shakshuka,** or a **Mediterranean grilled chicken platter**. These dishes are easy to scale up and typically don't require more time to prepare, even if you make double the quantity. Pair the main dish with a light **side salad** and a **simple dressing** to create a balanced meal. **Roasted vegetables, hummus,** and **pita bread** are great side dishes that are easy to prepare and perfect for sharing.

3. **Cooking for a Family**:
   When cooking for a family, Mediterranean meals can easily be made in large quantities. **Baked chicken with vegetables, fish tacos, couscous salads,** or **vegetable tagine** all work well as family-style dishes. **One-pan meals** or **sheet pan dinners**, where you roast everything together, are ideal for busy families. A **big pot of lentil soup** or **chickpea stew** can be made in advance and served for multiple meals. For dessert, make a batch of **Greek yogurt with honey and fruit** or **fruit sorbet** to share, providing a light and refreshing end to the meal.

By focusing on balance and simplicity, Mediterranean meals can easily adapt to different household sizes and ensure that everyone enjoys fresh, delicious, and nutritious food. Whether you're cooking for one or a family, the Mediterranean diet offers a variety of meals that are both satisfying and accessible.

stored in the fridge or freezer and quickly assembled into meals throughout the week. You can also pre-chop vegetables, marinate meats, or cook grains in bulk to streamline meal preparation. For example, you could prepare a large batch of **lentil stew** or **couscous salad** that can serve as a lunch or dinner option or roast a variety of **vegetables** to add to salads, grain bowls, or as sides for other dishes.

4. **Simple Meal Templates**:
   One of the easiest ways to maintain the Mediterranean diet is by following simple meal templates. For instance, create a **base** using whole grains or legumes, then add a **protein** (such as grilled chicken, fish, or beans), and top with **vegetables**, a drizzle of **olive oil**,

and a sprinkle of **herbs**. This basic formula can be customized with different ingredients each day, offering endless possibilities while keeping meals quick and easy to prepare.

Cooking for One, Two, or a Family: Adapting Mediterranean Meals for Every Need

One of the most appealing aspects of the Mediterranean diet is its flexibility, which allows it to be adapted for various household sizes and personal preferences. Whether you're cooking for one, two, or a whole family, the principles of Mediterranean cooking remain the same: use fresh, seasonal ingredients, prioritize plant-based foods, and enjoy meals that nourish both the body and soul.

1. **Cooking for One or Two**:
   When cooking for one or two people, the key is to keep things simple without making a lot of leftovers. Focus on **small portions** of fresh, high-quality ingredients. For example, make a **salad with roasted vegetables**, a handful of **quinoas**, and a **grilled chicken breast**, or prepare a quick stir-fry with **chickpeas**, **spinach**, and a drizzle of **olive oil**. Using smaller batches of grains or legumes allows for quick meals that can be prepared in under 30 minutes. You can also batch-cook individual portions, such as **single-serve vegetable frittatas** or **grain bowls**, that can be enjoyed throughout the week.
2. **Cooking for a Family**:
   When cooking for a family, Mediterranean meals are perfect for **family-style dining**. Dishes like **pasta, stews**, and **casseroles** are easy to scale up, providing a hearty meal that everyone can enjoy. Try making a large pot of **vegetable tagine, chicken and rice**, or a **big Greek salad** with **chickpeas** and **feta** that can feed several people. The beauty of Mediterranean cooking is that it doesn't require complicated recipes—simple, whole foods cooked together create rich and satisfying meals. Dishes like **paella** or **grilled fish with roasted vegetables** can easily feed a crowd, and many meals benefit from the communal aspect of sharing food.
3. **Flexibility for Special Diets**:
   The Mediterranean diet can be easily adapted for people with specific dietary needs, such as gluten-free, dairy-free, or vegetarian diets. If you're cooking for someone with dietary restrictions, simply swap out ingredients where needed. For example, substitute **gluten-free pasta** or **quinoa** in place of traditional pasta, or replace **cheese** with **nut-based cheeses** or a simple drizzle of **extra virgin olive oil**. The Mediterranean diet is naturally rich in **vegetables**, **legumes**, and **whole grains**, making it easy to find meals that suit a variety of needs.

THE MEDITERRANEAN LIFESTYLE

Chapter 17:

The Health Benefits of Mediterranean Eating

Improved Heart Health: How the Mediterranean Diet Promotes a Strong Heart

The Mediterranean diet is often hailed as one of the healthiest dietary patterns in the world, particularly for **heart health**. Rich in **monounsaturated fats** from **olive oil**, **omega-3 fatty acids** from fish, and an abundance of **antioxidant-rich fruits** and **vegetables**, this diet helps reduce the risk of **heart disease** and **stroke**. Studies have shown that individuals who follow the Mediterranean diet experience lower levels of **LDL (bad cholesterol)** and higher levels of **HDL (good cholesterol)**, as well as reduced blood pressure and improved **arterial function**.

1. **Olive Oil and Heart Health**:
   At the core of the Mediterranean diet is **extra virgin olive oil**, which has been extensively studied for its cardiovascular benefits. The **monounsaturated fats** in olive oil help lower harmful cholesterol levels, reduce inflammation, and prevent **oxidative stress**, all of which are major contributors to heart disease. **Polyphenols** found in olive oil, such as **oleocanthal**, also provide anti-inflammatory properties that help reduce the risk of chronic diseases.
2. **Omega-3 Fatty Acids from Fish**:
   Consuming fatty fish like **salmon**, **mackerel**, and **sardines** provides essential **omega-3 fatty acids**, which are linked to a lower incidence of heart disease. These healthy fats help lower **triglycerides**, reduce blood pressure, and prevent blood clots, making them vital for maintaining cardiovascular health.

Weight Loss and Management: The Role of Mediterranean Eating in Maintaining a Healthy Weight

While the Mediterranean diet isn't specifically designed for weight loss, its focus on whole, nutrient-dense foods, **portion control**, and **healthy fats** naturally leads to more balanced eating habits that can support weight management. The diet emphasizes **fiber-rich vegetables**, **legumes**, **whole grains**, and **lean proteins**, which promote satiety and prevent overeating.

1. **Satiety and Portion Control**:
   Many Mediterranean meals are packed with **fiber** from vegetables, **legumes**, and **whole grains**, which help you feel fuller for longer. **Protein-rich foods** like **fish**, **chicken**, and **beans** also contribute to feelings of fullness and help regulate **hunger hormones**, making it easier to maintain a healthy weight. Additionally, Mediterranean meals are typically prepared with healthy fats like olive oil, which help to balance **blood sugar** and reduce cravings.
2. **Balanced Macronutrients**:
   The Mediterranean diet emphasizes a balanced approach to **carbohydrates**, **proteins**, and **fats**, which helps stabilize blood sugar levels and reduce the risk of **insulin resistance**. This balance encourages the body to use energy efficiently, helping to prevent weight gain and promote fat burning. **Low-glycemic-index foods**, such as **whole grains** and **legumes**, are favored over refined sugars and processed foods, which can lead to weight gain.

Mental and Emotional Wellness: How Mediterranean Eating Can Improve Your Mood and Mind

Beyond physical health, the Mediterranean diet also plays a significant role in **mental well-being**. Research has shown that the Mediterranean diet, rich in **healthy fats**, **antioxidants**, and **omega-3s**, can support brain health, reduce the risk of **depression**, and even improve cognitive function.

1. **Brain-Boosting Nutrients**:
   Omega-3 fatty acids, found in fishlike **salmon**, **mackerel**, and **sardines**, are essential for brain health. These fats help maintain the structure and function of brain cells, improve mood regulation, and reduce the risk of **neurodegenerative diseases** like **Alzheimer's**. Additionally, the **polyphenols** in **olive oil**, **fruits**, and **vegetables** have been shown to reduce inflammation in the brain and protect against cognitive decline.
2. **Mood and Emotional Balance**:
   The Mediterranean diet also include foods known to support **mental health**, such as **leafy greens**, **berries**, and **whole grains**. These foods are rich in **folate**, **vitamin C**, and **vitamin B6**, which play important roles in the production of **serotonin**, the "feel-good" neurotransmitter. Consuming a variety of nutrient-dense foods has been linked to **lower levels of anxiety**, **improved mood**, and a reduced risk of **depression**. Furthermore, the

emphasis on **olive oil**, with its high levels of antioxidants, helps protect the brain from oxidative stress, which can negatively impact mood and mental health.

properties that help protect the heart by reducing inflammation in blood vessels. Studies, like those from the **PREDIMED study**, have consistently shown that a diet rich in olive oil can reduce the risk of **heart attacks**, **strokes**, and **death from heart disease** by a significant margin.

2. **Incorporating Fish and Omega-3 Fatty Acids**:
   Another pillar of the Mediterranean diet is **fish**, particularly oily fishlike **salmon**, **mackerel**, **sardines**, and **anchovies**, which are rich in **omega-3 fatty acids**. These healthy fats help reduce inflammation, lower triglyceride levels, and improve overall heart function. Omega-3s are known to prevent the buildup of **plaques** in the arteries and promote **vascular health**, further reducing the risk of **cardiovascular disease**.
3. **Plant-Based Diet for Heart Health**:
   The Mediterranean diet emphasizes a **plant-based** approach, with a heavy reliance on **fruits**, **vegetables**, **whole grains**, **nuts**, and **seeds**. These foods are rich in **fiber**, **vitamins**, and **minerals**, which support heart health by lowering blood pressure, reducing cholesterol, and improving overall circulation. The **antioxidants** in Mediterranean fruits, such as **berries**, **grapes**, and **pomegranates**, help combat oxidative damage to the cardiovascular system.

Weight Loss and Management: The Role of Mediterranean Eating in Maintaining a Healthy Weight

The Mediterranean diet is not only beneficial for heart health, but it is also incredibly effective for **weight loss** and **long-term weight management**. The focus on whole, minimally processed foods, healthy fats, and plant-based ingredients helps promote satiety, stabilize blood sugar levels, and reduce overall calorie intake.

1. **Sustainable, Balanced Eating**:
   Unlike fad diets that focus on drastic calorie restriction or eliminating entire food groups, the Mediterranean diet encourages a balanced approach to eating. By incorporating nutrient-dense foods like **fruits**, **vegetables**, **whole grains**, and **lean proteins**, it promotes **sustainable weight loss** without the need for severe deprivation. The diet encourages smaller portion sizes and emphasizes **moderation**, which is key to long-term weight management.
2. **Healthy Fats and Satiety**:
   One of the reasons the Mediterranean diet is so effective for weight management is its inclusion of **healthy fats**, particularly from **olive oil**, **avocados**, and **nuts**. These fats,

while calorie-dense, help keep you feeling full and satisfied, preventing overeating and reducing cravings. The diet's reliance on **protein-rich foods** like **fish**, **chicken**, and **legumes** also contributes to feelings of fullness, supporting healthier eating habits.

3. **Balanced Blood Sugar Levels**:
   The Mediterranean diet is naturally low in refined sugars and high in **fiber-rich whole foods**, both of which help regulate **blood sugar levels**. By promoting stable blood sugar levels, the diet helps prevent insulin spikes and crashes that can lead to overeating and weight gain. Studies show that the Mediterranean diet can significantly reduce the risk of **type 2 diabetes** and support healthy weight loss over time.

Mental and Emotional Wellness: How Mediterranean Eating Can Improve Your Mood and Mind

Mediterranean eating is not just beneficial for the body, but also for the **mind**. Research has shown that the Mediterranean diet may play a significant role in improving **mental health** and promoting **emotional well-being**. From reducing the risk of **depression** to improving **cognitive function**, the foods consumed in the Mediterranean diet support a healthy brain and emotional state.

1. **Anti-Inflammatory Effects and Mental Health**:
   Chronic **inflammation** has been linked to a variety of mental health disorders, including **depression** and **anxiety**. The Mediterranean diet is naturally anti-inflammatory, thanks to the high levels of **omega-3 fatty acids**, **polyphenols** (especially from olive oil and red wine), and **antioxidants** found in fruits and vegetables. By reducing inflammation in the brain, this diet may help reduce symptoms of depression, anxiety, and other mood disorders.
2. **Nutrient-Dense Foods for Cognitive Health**:
   The Mediterranean diet is rich in nutrients that support **cognitive function**. For example, **omega-3 fatty acids** found in fish play a critical role in brain health, helping improve **memory** and protect against cognitive decline. The diet's emphasis on **whole grains**, **nuts**, **leafy greens**, and **berries** provides essential vitamins and minerals—such as **vitamin E, folate**, and **magnesium**—that have been shown to support brain function and may help reduce the risk of **Alzheimer's disease** and **age-related cognitive decline**.
3. **Gut Health and Mood**:
   Emerging research has also highlighted the strong connection between **gut health** and **mental health**, often referred to as the "gut-brain axis." The Mediterranean diet's high fiber content, particularly from **legumes**, **whole grains**, and **fruits**, supports a healthy gut microbiome. A balanced gut microbiome can enhance the production of **serotonin** (the

"feel-good" hormone) and other neurotransmitters that regulate mood, leading to improved emotional well-being.

blood pressure, reducing **cholesterol levels**, and enhancing **blood vessel function**. **Fiber** from whole grains, fruits, and vegetables also helps to manage **blood sugar levels** and reduce the risk of **diabetes**, which is a significant risk factor for heart disease. Regular consumption of **nuts**, such as **almonds**, **walnuts**, and **pistachios**, has also been shown to improve heart health by providing a source of healthy fats, fiber, and plant-based protein.

By reducing processed foods and focusing on whole, nutrient-dense ingredients, the Mediterranean diet encourages heart-healthy eating that supports the body's ability to combat inflammation and oxidative stress, two major contributors to cardiovascular problems.

Weight Loss and Management: The Role of Mediterranean Eating in Maintaining a Healthy Weight

Maintaining a healthy weight is essential for overall well-being, and the Mediterranean diet provides an effective framework for sustainable weight loss and weight management. Unlike many fad diets that focus on restrictive eating patterns, the Mediterranean diet promotes a balanced, nutrient-rich approach that encourages healthy habits and long-term success.

1. **Balanced Meals and Portion Control**:
   The Mediterranean diet focuses on creating balanced meals that include a healthy combination of **protein, healthy fats, complex carbohydrates**, and **fiber**. This balance helps regulate **appetite** and **blood sugar levels**, reducing cravings and preventing overeating. For example, meals often include lean **protein** from fish, **legumes**, and **nuts**, as well as whole grains that provide long-lasting energy. The fiber in fruits, vegetables, and whole grains also promotes **satiety**, helping to curb hunger and reduce the tendency to overeat.
2. **Healthy Fats for Weight Management**:
   While many diets encourage avoiding fats to lose weight, the Mediterranean diet includes plenty of healthy **monounsaturated fats** from **olive oil** and **avocados**, as well as **omega-3 fatty acids** from fatty fish. These fats not only improve **heart health** but also promote a feeling of fullness, making it easier to manage portions and avoid unhealthy snacking. Studies show that people who consume moderate amounts of healthy fats tend to have better long-term success in weight management compared to those who follow very low-fat diets.
3. **Physical Activity and a Sustainable Lifestyle**:
   The Mediterranean lifestyle is not just about what you eat but also about staying active.

THE MEDITERRANEAN LIFESTYLE

Walking, **cycling**, and other forms of **moderate exercise** are deeply ingrained in Mediterranean culture, and this physical activity complements the diet in promoting weight management. This active lifestyle, combined with the Mediterranean diet's emphasis on balanced meals and portion control, leads to more sustainable weight loss without the need for drastic calorie restrictions or extreme dieting.

Mental and Emotional Wellness: How Mediterranean Eating Can Improve Your Mood and Mind

In addition to its physical health benefits, the Mediterranean diet can have a positive impact on **mental health** and **emotional wellness**. The foods that make up the Mediterranean diet are rich in **antioxidants, omega-3 fatty acids,** and **vitamins** that support brain health and emotional well-being.

1. **Omega-3 Fatty Acids for Brain Health**:
   As mentioned, **omega-3 fatty acids** from fish and **flaxseeds** are integral to the Mediterranean diet. These essential fats play a critical role in **brain function**, supporting cognitive abilities and reducing the risk of **cognitive decline** as we age. Studies have shown that a diet rich in omega-3s may help reduce symptoms of **depression** and **anxiety** by regulating neurotransmitters that influence mood.
2. **Antioxidants and Mental Clarity**:
   The Mediterranean diet is abundant in **antioxidant-rich foods**, such as **berries, dark leafy greens, tomatoes,** and **olive oil**. These antioxidants help reduce **oxidative stress** in the brain, which has been linked to cognitive decline and mood disorders. By fighting free radicals and reducing inflammation, these nutrient-dense foods contribute to mental clarity, improved memory, and a more positive outlook.
3. **Balanced Blood Sugar and Mood Regulation**:
   The Mediterranean diet's focus on **whole grains, legumes,** and **healthy fats** helps maintain **stable blood sugar levels**. This is important not only for physical health but also for **emotional well-being**. Fluctuating blood sugar levels can lead to mood swings, irritability, and energy crashes. By eating balanced meals that include healthy fats, fiber, and protein, the Mediterranean diet helps regulate blood sugar levels, leading to more stable moods and higher energy levels throughout the day.
4. **Social Connection and Mindful Eating**:
   Mediterranean eating is often a communal activity, with meals shared among family and friends. This emphasis on **social connections** and **mindful eating** contributes to **emotional wellness** by fostering feelings of happiness, community, and belonging. Studies have shown that eating meals with others, particularly in a relaxed, unhurried setting, can reduce stress and improve overall mental health. The Mediterranean approach

THE MEDITERRANEAN LIFESTYLE

encourages savoring food, enjoying the moment, and appreciating the sensory experience of eating, which can enhance overall well-being and satisfaction.

THE MEDITERRANEAN LIFESTYLE

Chapter 18:

Shopping and Sourcing Mediterranean Ingredients

Where to Find Fresh Mediterranean Ingredients: Farmers' Markets, Specialty Stores, and Online Sources

Sourcing the freshest, highest-quality Mediterranean ingredients is key to fully embracing the flavors and health benefits of this diet. The Mediterranean way of eating relies heavily on **seasonal, local** ingredients, which are often available at farmers' markets or through specialty stores. For ingredients that may be more difficult to find locally, online markets and international grocery stores can be excellent resources.

1. **Farmers' Markets**:
   Farmers' markets are a wonderful place to find fresh, seasonal produce that forms the backbone of the Mediterranean diet. Look for **leafy greens, tomatoes, cucumbers, peppers, eggplants,** and **herbs** like **oregano, parsley,** and **basil**. Many markets also offer a variety of **fruits**, such as **citrus, pomegranates,** and **stone fruits**, all of which play a prominent role in Mediterranean dishes. Additionally, you may be able to find **local olive oil** and artisan **cheeses**, which are often more flavorful and fresher than mass-produced options.
2. **Specialty Stores and Ethnic Markets**:
   For Mediterranean-specific ingredients, specialty stores or **ethnic markets** are an excellent resource. Stores that cater to **Middle Eastern, Greek, Italian,** or **Spanish** communities often carry items like **dried legumes** (lentils, chickpeas, beans), **figs, dried apricots, olives, couscous,** and **spices** like **sumac, cumin,** and **za'atar**. In addition, **Mediterranean spices** and **herbal blends**—such as **herbes de Provence, Turkish Baharat,** and **Saffron**—can be found in these specialty stores, elevating your cooking with authentic, vibrant flavors.
3. **Online Sources**:
   If you don't have access to a local Mediterranean market, online retailers have made it easier than ever to find authentic ingredients from all over the Mediterranean. Websites like **Amazon, Etsy, Mediterranean Foods,** and **herb** carry everything from high-quality

olive oil and **balsamic vinegar** to **spices**, **cheeses**, and even **fresh herbs**. Some specialty online grocers, like **The Mediterranean Dish** and **Greece's Best**, offer curated selections of **Greek olives**, **artisan olive oils**, and other unique items that you may not find locally.

Choosing Quality Products: Olive Oil, Cheese, and More

Quality matters when it comes to Mediterranean ingredients. The health benefits and flavor of the Mediterranean diet are closely linked to the quality of the ingredients you use, especially **olive oil**, **cheese**, and other core products. Here's how to choose the best:

1. **Olive Oil**:
   Extra virgin olive oil (EVOO) is the cornerstone of Mediterranean cooking. When shopping for olive oil, look for oils labeled **cold-pressed** or **first cold-pressed**, as these are the highest quality. EVOO should have a rich, greenish color, a robust flavor, and a slightly **peppery** finish. It's best to choose **small-batch**, **single-origin** oils whenever possible, as they tend to offer more nuanced flavors. Always check the **harvest date**—the fresher the olive oil, the better it will taste and the more antioxidants it will contain. Keep your olive oil stored in a cool, dark place to preserve its freshness.

2. **Cheese**:
   Mediterranean cheeses are varied and delicious, with each country offering its own unique styles. **Feta** from **Greece**, **Manchego** from **Spain**, and **pecorino** from **Italy** are just a few examples of the cheeses that play a central role in Mediterranean dishes. When choosing cheese, look for **artisan, small-batch** varieties, as they often have more complex flavors. **Aged cheeses** like **pecorino** or **Parmigiano-Reggiano** are excellent for grating over pastas, salads, and soups. When shopping for **feta**, look for versions made with **sheep's milk** or a blend of **sheep's and goat's milk**—they tend to have a richer, creamier texture.

3. **Fresh Produce**:
   Mediterranean cuisine emphasizes **seasonal, locally grown produce**, and the fresher your ingredients, the better your dishes will taste. **Organic** produce is a good choice when available, as it tends to have more flavor and fewer pesticides. Look for **tomatoes**, **eggplants**, **zucchini**, **peppers**, and **greens** that are vibrant in color and firm to the touch. For **herbs**, opt for fresh over dried whenever possible, as they add a bright, aromatic flavor that dried versions often lack.

4. **Herbs and Spices**:
   Fresh herbs like **oregano**, **rosemary**, **thyme**, and **basil** are essential for creating authentic Mediterranean flavors. If fresh herbs are unavailable, **dried herbs** can work in a pinch, but always choose **high-quality** ones. When it comes to **spices**, opt for **whole**

THE MEDITERRANEAN LIFESTYLE

spices whenever possible, as they tend to have more flavor than pre-ground varieties. **Saffron**, **sumac**, **cumin**, and **paprika** are just a few of the key spices that make Mediterranean dishes so aromatic.

authentic than mass-produced varieties. Farmers' markets also offer an opportunity to support **local producers** and source **organic** or **sustainably grown** ingredients, which are central to the Mediterranean ethos of eating whole, minimally processed foods.

5. **Specialty Stores**:
   For more unique Mediterranean ingredients, **specialty grocery stores** or **ethnic markets** are invaluable. These stores typically carry a wide selection of **Mediterranean staples** like **olive oils, aged vinegars, spices, dried legumes,** and **artisanal cheeses**. In larger cities, you might find stores that specifically cater to Mediterranean or Middle Eastern communities, where you can find items such as **harissa**, **tahini**, **za'atar**, **sumac**, and **figs**. **Mediterranean bakeries** and delicatessens can also be great places to pick up **pita**, **baklava**, or **flatbreads**.

6. **Online Sources**:
   If you're unable to find specific Mediterranean ingredients locally, online shopping is an excellent option. There are several reputable websites that specialize in importing high-quality Mediterranean foods, such as **Etsy, Amazon,** and **Mediterranean Direct**, where you can purchase products like **extra virgin olive oil**, **feta cheese**, **couscous**, and **preserved lemons**. **Olive oil subscription services** and **importers of fine wines** can also help you discover top-tier products from Mediterranean regions. Additionally, **specialty spice companies** offer authentic spices like **saffron**, **cumin**, **coriander**, and **turmeric**, which are staples in Mediterranean cooking.

7. **Ethnic and Mediterranean Grocery Chains**:
   If you're in a city with a larger international community, you might have access to grocery chains that specialize in Mediterranean or Middle Eastern foods. These stores typically carry a variety of **breads, cheeses, olives,** and **pickles**, along with **pre-marinated meats** for grilling and cooking.

Choosing Quality Products: Olive Oil, Cheese, and More

The Mediterranean diet revolves around the use of a few high-quality ingredients, and selecting the best of these can significantly enhance the flavors and nutritional benefits of your meals. Here's how to choose the highest quality products for your Mediterranean kitchen.

1. **Olive Oil**:
   Extra virgin olive oil (EVOO) is the cornerstone of Mediterranean cooking, known for

THE MEDITERRANEAN LIFESTYLE

its rich flavor and health benefits. When purchasing olive oil, always look for **cold-pressed** or **first-press** oils, as these retain the most nutrients and flavor. Choose oils labeled as **extra virgin**, as they are less processed and contain more antioxidants. **Dark glass bottles** or **tins** are preferable because they protect the oil from light and oxidation. For everyday cooking, you can find excellent quality olive oils from **Italy**, **Spain**, **Greece**, and **Tunisia**, but look for one that has been harvested in the **current year** for optimal freshness. For a more robust flavor, opt for oils from regions like **Tuscany** or **Sicily**, which are known for their rich, peppery oils.

2. **Cheese**:

Mediterranean cheeses are diverse and range from creamy and mild to tangy and sharp. Look for **authentic** cheeses such as **feta** (Greece), **Manchego** (Spain), **pecorino Romano** (Italy), and **halloumi** (Cyprus). When shopping for cheese, always opt for **artisan** or **PDO** (Protected Designation of Origin) products, as these are made using traditional methods and represent the true flavors of the region. For **feta**, choose one that is stored in brine for the best flavor, and for **Manchego**, look for aged varieties with a firm, nutty texture.

3. **Herbs and Spices**:

The Mediterranean diet is known for its **herb-forward** cooking. Fresh herbs like **oregano**, **rosemary**, **thyme**, and **basil** are essential to Mediterranean flavor. If you're purchasing dried herbs, ensure they are **organic** and **freshly dried**, as older dried herbs can lose much of their flavor. For spices, Mediterranean staples like **paprika**, **cumin**, **sumac**, and **saffron** bring complexity to the food. **Saffron** should be purchased in **threads**, not powdered form, for the most potent flavor and color.

4. **Fish and Seafood**:

Fresh seafood is an integral part of Mediterranean cuisine, especially in coastal areas. When buying fish, look for varieties that are locally sourced and **sustainably caught**. Ideally, you want to buy fish that is as **fresh** as possible, ideally from local markets or trusted **seafood vendors**. Fish like **sardines**, **mackerel**, and **anchovies** are particularly common in Mediterranean diets and can often be purchased canned or preserved in **olive oil** for convenience.

5. **Legumes, Grains, and Pasta**:

Mediterranean diets incorporate many **legumes** and **whole grains**, such as **chickpeas**, **lentils**, **quinoa**, and **farro**. When purchasing these, look for varieties that are **whole** and minimally processed. For pasta, traditional **Italian pasta** made with **durum wheat semolina** is ideal, and pasta made from **whole grains** or **ancient grains** like **farro** or **spelt** offers an added nutritional boost.

By sourcing the best-quality ingredients, whether through farmers' markets, specialty stores, or online, you'll be able to fully embrace the authentic Mediterranean experience—one that celebrates fresh, vibrant, and healthy foods.

THE MEDITERRANEAN LIFESTYLE

THE MEDITERRANEAN LIFESTYLE

Chapter 19:

Mediterranean Lifestyle Beyond the Plate

Active Living: Mediterranean Fitness and Outdoor Activities

The Mediterranean lifestyle isn't just about what you eat—it's about living a balanced, active life that incorporates physical movement, connection with nature, and time spent outdoors. In Mediterranean cultures, staying active and enjoying outdoor activities is as much a part of daily life as the food they consume. Here's how you can integrate the Mediterranean approach to fitness and outdoor living into your own routine:

1. **Walking and Everyday Movement**:
   In Mediterranean countries, especially in rural areas or small towns, **walking** is a daily activity. People walk to work, to the market, and even to visit family and friends. This routine encourages consistent movement, which is essential for overall health. Walking is not only good for cardiovascular health but also helps with weight management, mental well-being, and maintaining a connection to the local community.
2. **Outdoor Activities and Leisure**:
   The Mediterranean climate, with its warm, sunny weather, makes outdoor activities a joy. **Swimming**, **hiking**, **cycling**, and **playing sports** are all common ways to stay fit in the region. In coastal areas, water-based activities like **kayaking**, **sailing**, or simply enjoying the beach are popular forms of exercise and relaxation. In more rural areas, people may engage in farming or gardening, providing them with both physical activity and the satisfaction of growing their own food. These activities not only improve physical health but also foster a deeper connection to nature and a sense of well-being.
3. **Yoga and Meditation**:
   While the Mediterranean diet is well known, Mediterranean cultures also emphasize **mental wellness** through practices like **yoga**, **tai chi**, and **meditation**. These practices, which promote mindfulness and relaxation, complement the region's active lifestyle. The calming atmosphere and connection to the natural world in Mediterranean environments make it an ideal place for mental and emotional restoration, further enhancing the holistic approach to health.

THE MEDITERRANEAN LIFESTYLE

The Mediterranean Approach to Socializing: Dining, Family, and Community

In Mediterranean cultures, food is more than just nourishment—it is a central aspect of **socializing, family gatherings**, and **community life**. Sharing a meal is an opportunity to bond with loved ones, celebrate life's milestones, and strengthen relationships. Here's a look at how the Mediterranean approach to socializing can enrich your own life:

1. **Family Meals and Social Dining**:
   Family meals are a cornerstone of the Mediterranean way of life. Whether it's a **lunch** or **dinner**, eating together is seen as an essential ritual for connecting with family members and building strong relationships. Meals are typically shared **family-style**, with a variety of dishes placed in the center of the table, encouraging conversation and collaboration. In Mediterranean cultures, it's not uncommon for meals to last for several hours, with courses spread out over time to allow for relaxation and connection.
2. **Socializing Around the Table**:
   Dining in the Mediterranean is often a social affair. **Friends, neighbors**, and **extended family** frequently gather to share food and drinks, creating a sense of community. This practice not only fosters social connections but also emphasizes the importance of **slowing down** and enjoying the present moment. Whether it's sharing **meze** in Greece, a **barbecue** in Spain, or a **feast** in Italy, these social gatherings are an essential part of Mediterranean life.
3. **Celebrating Special Occasions**:
   The Mediterranean way of life also places great importance on celebrating special events with food. **Weddings, birthdays**, and **holidays** are often marked by large gatherings and extravagant meals. In some regions, it's customary to spend several days preparing for and celebrating these events, ensuring that everyone has the chance to participate. These celebrations are not just about food—they are about **community, connection**, and sharing joy with others.
4. **The Role of Wine and Olive Oil in Social Settings**:
   No Mediterranean gathering is complete without **wine** or **olive oil**—two symbols of the region's culture. Wine is often enjoyed with family and friends, especially during meals, where it acts as both a drink and a social lubricant, encouraging conversation and bonding. Olive oil, on the other hand, is a symbol of hospitality and abundance. It is used not just in cooking but also as a gesture of goodwill when served to guests, emphasizing the Mediterranean values of **generosity** and **sharing**.

THE MEDITERRANEAN LIFESTYLE

surfing, **kayaking**, and **sailing** are popular, while those in more mountainous regions enjoy **hiking**, **rock climbing**, and **trail running**. The Mediterranean lifestyle encourages a love for nature, whether it's walking through vineyards in **Italy**, cycling along the coast in **Greece**, or swimming in the crystal-clear waters of the **Aegean Sea**. Regular exposure to fresh air and physical activity not only improves physical health but also enhances mood and mental clarity.

3. **Farming and Gardening**:
   Many Mediterranean communities also stay active through **farming** or **gardening**. Growing their own produce—whether it's **herbs**, **vegetables**, or **fruit trees**—is a common and cherished practice. This connection to the earth not only provides fresh, seasonal ingredients but also promotes physical labor that benefits strength and flexibility. Plus, gardening has been shown to reduce stress, increase happiness, and improve overall well-being.

By incorporating these active living principles, you can embrace the Mediterranean lifestyle by finding ways to integrate movement into your daily routine—whether through structured workouts or simply by spending more time outside.

The Mediterranean Approach to Socializing: Dining, Family, and Community

The Mediterranean way of life is deeply social, and meals are seen not just as a chance to nourish the body but as an opportunity to connect with loved ones and the community. Dining in the Mediterranean is often a communal activity, rich in conversation, laughter, and bonding.

1. **Family-Centered Meals**:
   In Mediterranean cultures, meals are often shared with family, friends, and extended loved ones. There's a strong emphasis on **togetherness**, where families gather around the table to enjoy fresh, home-cooked meals. These meals tend to be leisurely, lasting for several hours, with conversation flowing freely between courses. The **family meal** is not just about food—it's about building relationships, passing on traditions, and strengthening familial bonds. Sharing a meal is a ritual that deepens connections and fosters a sense of belonging.
2. **Community and Social Events**:
   Socializing is central to Mediterranean life, and food is often at the heart of these gatherings. From **street festivals** in **Spain** and **Greece** to **family BBQs** in **Italy** and **Turkey**, there are many opportunities for communal dining and celebrating. **Tapas**, **meze**, and **buffets** are popular ways to serve food in a social setting, allowing everyone to share a variety of small dishes. In many Mediterranean countries, it's not uncommon

THE MEDITERRANEAN LIFESTYLE

for neighbors to gather for **potlucks** or **picnics**, where everyone contributes a dish, making the meal a reflection of community spirit.

3. **Slowing Down and Enjoying the Moment**:
   A key part of Mediterranean social life is the idea of **slowing down** and savoring the moment. This is known as the **"slow food"** philosophy, where meals are prepared and enjoyed without rush. People take time to appreciate the flavors, enjoy the company of others, and connect with the rhythms of life. In the Mediterranean, eating is not just about filling the stomach—it's a time for relaxation, reflection, and nurturing relationships. This slower, more mindful approach to dining encourages a deeper connection to both food and community.

4. **Celebrations and Rituals**:
   Every region in the Mediterranean has its own food-related traditions that accompany festivals, holidays, and rituals. For example, in **Italy**, families gather for a big **Christmas Eve feast**, while **Greece** celebrates **Easter** with traditional lamb and sweets. In **Morocco**, elaborate feasts accompany major life events like weddings and baptisms. These occasions are not just about food; they represent the coming together of community and culture. Sharing these meals strengthens a sense of belonging and identity within the broader Mediterranean society.

By embracing this communal and slow-paced approach to meals, you can create more meaningful moments with your own family and friends, leading to deeper connections and richer social experiences.

Community

The Mediterranean lifestyle is deeply rooted in **connection**—to family, friends, and the community. Socializing is an integral part of life, and meals are often seen as a time not only to nourish the body but also to nourish relationships. In Mediterranean cultures, dining is a communal activity, a chance to share stories, celebrate milestones, and bond over a shared appreciation for food. Here's how the Mediterranean approach to socializing can enrich your life:

1. **Family-Centered Meals**:
   Meals in Mediterranean households are typically family affairs. Whether it's a **Sunday lunch** or a casual dinner during the week, families gather around the table to enjoy food together. These meals are often leisurely, lasting several hours, with multiple courses that encourage conversation and connection. The Mediterranean way of dining emphasizes **sharing**, which fosters a sense of community and togetherness. It's not just about eating—it's about enjoying each other's company, engaging in meaningful conversations, and creating lasting memories.

THE MEDITERRANEAN LIFESTYLE

2. **The Ritual of the Shared Meal**:
   In many Mediterranean cultures, **family-style dining** is the norm. Platters of food are placed in the center of the table, and everyone serves themselves, allowing for a dynamic, interactive dining experience. The act of sharing food brings people closer together, and often, meals are complemented by **laughter**, **stories**, and **celebrations**. This practice helps strengthen bonds and create a sense of belonging. Meals are also often a time for **hospitality**, where guests are warmly invited to join in the feast, reflecting the Mediterranean ethos of **generosity**.

3. **Outdoor Socializing and Al Fresco Dining**:
   With the abundance of **sunshine** and temperate weather, the Mediterranean lifestyle emphasizes outdoor dining. Whether it's a casual meal on the balcony, a family gathering in the garden, or a community celebration at the beach, dining al fresco is a cherished tradition. The connection to nature during meals enhances the experience, creating an atmosphere of relaxation and enjoyment. It's common to see long tables laden with dishes of fresh salads, grilled fish, roasted meats, and vibrant vegetables, all shared among friends and family.

4. **Celebrations and Festivals**:
   Throughout the Mediterranean, **festivals** and **celebrations** are regular occurrences, often centered around food, music, and dance. These events serve not only to honor traditions but also to come together as a community. From **harvest festivals** in Spain to **feasts** celebrating saints in Italy and **weddings** in Greece, food plays a central role in these gatherings. These celebrations often involve long meals, with traditional dishes served in abundance, where the focus is on enjoyment, socializing, and creating shared experiences.

5. **The Role of Wine and Spirits in Socializing**:
   In the Mediterranean, **wine** is often more than just a drink—it's a social lubricant, enhancing the experience of sharing a meal. Wine is often enjoyed in moderation, as part of a leisurely meal, with the flavors of the wine complementing the dishes served. Similarly, local **spirits** like **ouzo** (Greece), **raki** (Turkey), and **grappa** (Italy) are often enjoyed in small quantities as part of celebrations or after-dinner rituals. These drinks are typically served in a **ritualistic** manner, adding a cultural dimension to the socializing process. They invite guests to linger at the table and continue conversations long after the meal is over.

6. **Mediterranean Friendships and Community Spirit**:
   In Mediterranean countries, there's a strong sense of **community** that extends beyond the family. Neighbors, friends, and even strangers often come together to share meals, help one another, and celebrate life. The concept of **community** is deeply embedded in Mediterranean culture, and it is not uncommon to see large groups gathering for **barbecues**, **feasts**, or **local festivals**. This sense of belonging and collective enjoyment

THE MEDITERRANEAN LIFESTYLE

plays a vital role in mental and emotional well-being, fostering a deep connection to others and to the community.

By embracing the Mediterranean approach to socializing, you can enrich your own life by fostering stronger relationships, building a sense of community, and creating lasting memories around the dining table. The Mediterranean way is not just about eating healthy food—it's about **living well**, with love, laughter, and connection at the heart of every meal.

THE MEDITERRANEAN LIFESTYLE

Chapter 20:

Adapting the Mediterranean Diet to Your Own Taste

Personalizing Mediterranean Dishes: Adjusting Recipes to Fit Your Preferences

One of the best aspects of the **Mediterranean diet** is its flexibility. It's not a one-size-fits-all approach—it's a framework that can be adapted to suit your personal tastes, dietary preferences, and lifestyle. Whether you're vegan, gluten-free, or prefer lighter meals, you can easily personalize Mediterranean dishes to suit your needs while staying true to the core principles of the diet.

1. **Substituting Ingredients**:
   While the Mediterranean diet emphasizes certain core ingredients—**olive oil**, **seafood**, **whole grains**, **vegetables**, and **legumes**—you can make substitutions based on what you like or what's available in your local area. For example:
   - If you're not a fan of **eggplant**, try using **zucchini** or **mushrooms** in dishes like **moussaka** or **caponata**.
   - **Chickpeas** can be swapped with **lentils** in salads or stews for a different texture, or you can substitute **quinoa** for **couscous** for a gluten-free option.
   - For a dairy-free alternative to **feta cheese**, try using **tofu** marinated in olive oil, lemon, and oregano, or **vegan cheese** made from nuts like cashews.
2. **Adjusting Flavor Profiles**:
   Mediterranean cuisine is known for its fresh, bold flavors, but you can easily adjust the **seasonings** and **herbs** to fit your preferences. Love heat? Add more **red pepper flakes**, **harissa**, or **fresh chilies** to your dishes. Prefer milder flavors? Use a light hand with **garlic** and **onions** and opt for **fresh herbs** like **parsley** and **basil** instead of more pungent spices.
   Experimenting with flavors can also involve swapping ingredients based on your culinary cravings. For instance, if you're making a **Greek salad** but want to change up the traditional **cucumber** or **tomato**, try adding **avocado, pomegranate seeds**, or **grilled peaches** for a modern twist on the classic.

THE MEDITERRANEAN LIFESTYLE

Creating Your Own Mediterranean Recipes: How to Experiment and Explore

While traditional Mediterranean recipes are timeless, the beauty of the diet lies in its versatility and its encouragement of **creativity**. You don't need to stick strictly to the "classic" recipes to enjoy Mediterranean-inspired meals—feel free to **experiment, explore new combinations**, and **create your own** dishes based on the principles of Mediterranean cuisine. Here's how:

1. **Start with a Mediterranean Foundation**:
   Begin by focusing on the basic elements of Mediterranean cuisine. Think of **healthy fats** (like **olive oil** or **avocados**), **whole grains** (such as **farro**, **brown rice**, or **quinoa**), **lean proteins** (like **chicken**, **fish**, or **beans**), and **fresh vegetables** (like **tomatoes**, **cucumbers**, **spinach**, and **eggplant**). Once you have these core ingredients, you can build your meals around them. For example, you can create a Mediterranean-inspired **grain bowl** by mixing cooked grains with grilled vegetables, a protein (like **chickpeas** or **grilled salmon**), and a drizzle of olive oil and tahini.

2. **Use Mediterranean Cooking Techniques**:
   Embrace Mediterranean cooking methods like **grilling**, **roasting**, **slow-braising**, and **sauteing** to bring out the natural flavors of the ingredients. You can experiment with grilling **vegetables** or **fruit** for added smokiness, or slow-cooking **stews** and **tagines** to develop deep, rich flavors. Even a simple dish like **roasted vegetables** can become exciting when seasoned with the right spices like **oregano**, **paprika**, and **garlic**, and finished with a drizzle of **extra virgin olive oil**.

3. **Play with Mediterranean Flavors and Combinations**:
   The Mediterranean diet is rich in **herbs**, **spices**, and **seasonings** that elevate the flavor profile of any dish. When creating your own Mediterranean recipes, don't hesitate to play with different combinations of these elements. Try adding **cumin** and **coriander** to a **vegetable stew**, or **rosemary** and **thyme** to **roasted potatoes**. **Lemon** and **oregano** can be a simple but powerful marinade for **grilled meats**, while **mint** and **parsley** can refresh and brighten up salads or dips.

4. **Adapt to Your Dietary Preferences**:
   Whether you follow a specific **dietary regimen** (such as **vegan**, **gluten-free**, or **low-carb**) or have personal preferences, Mediterranean cuisine can easily be adapted to fit. For example, you can create **vegan Mediterranean dishes** by swapping out dairy or meat products for plant-based options, such as **tofu**, **tempeh**, or **seitan**, and using **nut-based cheeses** like cashew cheese in place of traditional **feta** or **ricotta**. Similarly, you can experiment with **gluten-free grains** like **quinoa**, **rice**, or **polenta** in place of **pasta** or **bread**.

couscous in grain-based dishes like **tabbouleh** or **paella**.

2. **Customizing Flavor Profiles**:
   Mediterranean cuisine is known for its **fresh herbs**, **spices**, and **citrus**. You can adjust the seasonings in any dish to suit your taste. If you love the vibrant flavor of **coriander**, add it to your **tabbouleh** or **hummus**. Prefer something milder? Use **parsley** or **basil** for a more subdued flavor profile. Similarly, if you enjoy a bit of **heat**, consider incorporating **cayenne pepper** or **chili flakes** to spice up dishes like **gazpacho** or **shakshuka**.
3. **Vegetarian or Meat-Lover's Adaptation**:
   Many Mediterranean recipes are naturally plant-based, but if you prefer a protein boost, you can always add **grilled chicken**, **fish**, or **lamb** to salads, grain bowls, or pastas. If you're vegan, experiment with **tofu** or **tempeh** as substitutes for dairy or meat in dishes like **Greek salad** or **spanakopita**. The Mediterranean diet offers an abundance of options, making it easy to adapt the dishes to your protein needs.
4. **Gluten-Free or Low-Carb Modifications**:
   If you're following a **gluten-free** or **low-carb** lifestyle, the Mediterranean diet offers a wealth of options. Instead of traditional **pasta**, you can opt for **zucchini noodles**, **spiralized vegetables**, or **cauliflower rice**. You can also swap **bread** for **gluten-free** versions or skip it altogether in **meze** or **appetizer** spreads.

By experimenting with ingredients and flavors that resonate with your personal preferences, you can enjoy the Mediterranean diet in a way that works best for you without compromising on taste or nutrition.

Creating Your Own Mediterranean Recipes: How to Experiment and Explore

The beauty of Mediterranean cuisine is that it thrives on creativity and **seasonal ingredients**, which means there's always room to experiment and make dishes your own. Here are some ways to explore and create your own Mediterranean-inspired recipes:

1. **Incorporating Seasonal Produce**:
   Mediterranean cooking celebrates the **seasons**, so a great place to start is by creating dishes based on what's in season. Visit your local farmers' market, or check out your grocery store's seasonal produce section, and build your recipes around these ingredients. For example, in **summer**, you might create a **tomato and watermelon salad** with fresh **basil** and **feta**, while in **winter**, a hearty **root vegetable stew** with **chickpeas** and **spices** could be the perfect meal.
2. **Experimenting with Mediterranean Staples**:
   Try creating your own spin on classic Mediterranean dishes. If you're a fan of **pasta**, you could create a unique Mediterranean-inspired dish by pairing it with **artichokes**, **sun-**

THE MEDITERRANEAN LIFESTYLE

> **dried tomatoes**, and **olives**, drizzled with a lemony **garlic olive oil sauce**. If you love **couscous**, consider adding roasted **vegetables** and a simple dressing made of **yogurt** and **tahini**.

3. **Blending Mediterranean with Other Cuisines**:
   Feel free to mix Mediterranean principles with flavors from other culinary traditions. For instance, you could combine the Mediterranean love for **grilled vegetables** and **olive oil** with **Asian-inspired** spices like **ginger** and **sesame** to create a fusion dish like **Mediterranean sesame-crusted grilled veggies**. Or blend the flavors of the Mediterranean with **Mexican** ingredients, like using **avocado** and **lime** in a fresh **Greek salad** or turning **hummus** into a delicious dip with a hint of **cilantro** and **lime**.

4. **Embrace the Mediterranean Way of Cooking**:
   As you begin to create your own recipes, remember that Mediterranean cooking is all about simplicity. Don't overcomplicate things—use **fresh, high-quality ingredients** and allow their natural flavors to shine. Whether you're crafting a new **grain bowl**, a hearty **stew**, or a fresh **salad**, focus on the balance of flavors, textures, and colors that make Mediterranean cuisine so vibrant.

By following these principles, you can create a Mediterranean-inspired menu that reflects your own unique taste, while still staying true to the core values of fresh, healthy, and delicious food. Experiment, have fun with it, and don't be afraid to make the recipes your own!

stuffed grape leaves (dolma). For those who are dairy-free, you can replace traditional cheeses like **feta** with plant-based options or simply omit cheese from salads and pasta dishes. The Mediterranean diet's inherent flexibility makes it easy to create meals that cater to **vegetarian**, **vegan**, or **paleo** preferences without sacrificing flavor.

4. **Adjusting for Allergies or Sensitivities**:
   If you have specific dietary restrictions, such as gluten or dairy intolerance, the Mediterranean diet is relatively easy to adjust. For example:
   - **Gluten-Free**: You can swap **traditional pasta** with gluten-free varieties made from **rice, corn**, or **quinoa**. **Polenta, rice, quinoa**, or **buckwheat** also work well as gluten-free grains in Mediterranean dishes like **risotto** or **paella**.
   - **Dairy-Free**: If you're avoiding dairy, many Mediterranean dishes naturally cater to this. For example, **olive oil-based** dips like **hummus** and **tzatziki** (made with **almond yogurt** or **coconut yogurt** as a substitute) are delicious alternatives that require no dairy at all.

5. **Sweeteners and Healthy Swaps**:
   The Mediterranean diet emphasizes **natural sweeteners** like **honey** and **dates**. If you're looking for ways to satisfy your sweet tooth without refined sugars, **date syrup, maple syrup**, or a sprinkle of **cinnamon** can be used in desserts or breakfast dishes. For a

THE MEDITERRANEAN LIFESTYLE

healthy dessert alternative, try baked **fruit** like **apples** or **pears**, drizzled with **olive oil** and **honey**, and topped with crushed **almonds** or **walnuts**.

Creating Your Own Mediterranean Recipes: How to Experiment and Explore

While Mediterranean recipes come with centuries of tradition and time-tested combinations, part of the fun of this diet is its flexibility for **creativity** and **personal experimentation**. Here's how you can explore and create your own Mediterranean-inspired dishes:

1. **Start with Classic Foundations**:
   Begin by mastering the basic dishes that form the backbone of Mediterranean cuisine, such as **salads, grilled meats, grain bowls**, and **vegetable-based stews**. Once you're comfortable with the flavor combinations, you can begin experimenting with adding your own spin to these dishes.
   - For example, create a **grain bowl** with **quinoa, roasted vegetables, grilled chicken, hummus**, and a **lemon-tahini dressing**.
   - Or experiment with different **pasta sauces** using tomatoes, **basil, garlic**, and **olive oil**, but with a twist—add **sun-dried tomatoes** or **olives** for a more complex flavor.
2. **Embrace Seasonal Produce**:
   Mediterranean cuisine thrives on seasonal ingredients, so make it a habit to visit your local farmers' market or grocery store each season to discover what's available. Whether it's fresh **tomatoes** in summer, **squash** in fall, or **citrus** in winter, these ingredients can inspire entirely new dishes. You can create unique **seasonal soups, salads**, or **pasta dishes** that highlight the produce available at different times of the year.
3. **Experiment with Mediterranean Fusion**:
   The beauty of Mediterranean cooking is its ability to **blend** with other culinary traditions. Try **fusion dishes** that incorporate Mediterranean ingredients with flavors from other regions of the world. For example, mix the richness of **Mediterranean olive oil** and **herbs** with the spice of **Indian curry**, or combine **Middle Eastern hummus** with **Mexican tacos** for a fun and flavorful twist.
4. **Keep the Essentials but Play with Presentation**:
   Mediterranean food is often simple and rustic, but you can elevate your presentation by using creative plating, vibrant garnishes, and fresh herbs. Whether it's **chickpea stew**, a simple **grilled fish**, or a classic **tabbouleh**, try arranging your dishes in a way that's visually appealing. Adding colorful elements such as **pomegranate seeds, edible flowers**, or a **sprig of rosemary** can give your Mediterranean-inspired meals a gourmet touch.

THE MEDITERRANEAN LIFESTYLE

5. **Listen to Your Taste Buds**:
   The beauty of Mediterranean cooking is that it's all about balance—balance of flavors, textures, and ingredients. Don't be afraid to experiment and taste your way through recipes. Add **extra garlic** if you love its bold flavor or try a **splash of red wine vinegar** for added acidity in your salad dressings. The more you cook, the more you'll develop a deep understanding of what works for your own palate.

Embracing the Mediterranean diet doesn't mean adhering strictly to traditional recipes—it's about adapting and personalizing meals to suit your preferences while maintaining the core principles of **fresh, whole ingredients**, **healthy fats**, and a **balanced lifestyle**. By experimenting with different ingredients, flavors, and techniques, you can create Mediterranean-inspired dishes that are uniquely your own.

THE MEDITERRANEAN LIFESTYLE

Appendices

Conversion Tables: Metric vs. Imperial Measurements

Cooking in the Mediterranean tradition often involves using both **metric** and **imperial** measurement systems, depending on where you're located. To make your cooking experience seamless, here's a quick reference guide for converting common measurements.

Ingredient	Metric	Imperial
Water	1 liter	4.2 cups
Olive oil	1 tablespoon	0.5 fluid ounce
Flour	100 grams	3.5 ounces
Sugar	100 grams	3.5 ounces
Salt	1 teaspoon	0.2 teaspoon
Butter	1 stick (113g)	1/2 cup
Eggs	1 large egg	1 large egg
Ground spices (e.g., cumin, paprika)	1 teaspoon	1 teaspoon

Note: The Mediterranean diet emphasizes using fresh, local, and seasonal ingredients, so always check the packaging of items you purchase, especially for **weights and volumes**.

Index of Mediterranean Ingredients and Recipes

This index provides an easy way to locate key ingredients and their corresponding recipes in the book, ensuring you can quickly find the elements that interest you most.

A

- **Aged Balsamic Vinegar** – Chapter 5, Mediterranean Salads and Sides, p. 120
- **Anchovies** – Chapter 9, Seafood and Fish, p. 211

B

THE MEDITERRANEAN LIFESTYLE

- **Baklava** – Chapter 13, Mediterranean Desserts, p. 275
- **Basil** – Chapter 7, Salads and Sides, p. 135
- **Bulgur** – Chapter 11, Pasta and Grains, p. 188

C

- **Chickpeas** – Chapter 6, Appetizers and Small Plates, p. 156
- **Couscous** – Chapter 11, Pasta and Grains, p. 190

D

- **Dolma (Stuffed Grape Leaves)** – Chapter 6, Appetizers and Small Plates, p. 168

Glossary of Mediterranean Cooking Terms

Mediterranean cooking is rich with specific terminology that might be unfamiliar to some. Here's a helpful guide to understand key terms used throughout this book.

- **Al Dente** (Italian): A term used to describe pasta or vegetables that are cooked so they still have a firm bite.
- **Antipasto** (Italian): A traditional Italian appetizer that often includes **cured meats**, **cheese**, **olives**, **marinated vegetables**, and **bread**.
- **Baba Ghanoush** (Middle Eastern): A smoky, creamy dip made from **eggplant**, **tahini**, **olive oil**, **garlic**, and **lemon juice**.
- **Couscous** (North African): A traditional dish made from steamed **semolina wheat** grains, often served as a side or mixed with vegetables, meats, or sauces.
- **Frittata** (Italian): An Italian-style omelet that is often made with vegetables, cheese, and sometimes **meats**, and is cooked slowly on the stove.
- **Harissa** (North African): A spicy paste made from **chili peppers**, **garlic**, **coriander**, **caraway**, and **olive oil**.
- **Tagine** (Moroccan): A traditional **Moroccan stew** made with **meat**, **vegetables**, and **spices**, slow cooked in a **clay pot** with a conical lid.
- **Za'atar** (Middle Eastern): A blend of **dried thyme**, **oregano**, **marjoram**, **sumac**, **sesame seeds**, and **salt**, commonly used as a seasoning or a condiment.

These terms will help guide your cooking experience and ensure that you understand the ingredients and methods used in Mediterranean dishes.

Ingredient	Metric	Imperial

THE MEDITERRANEAN LIFESTYLE

Ingredient	Metric	Imperial
Butter	1 stick (113g)	1/2 cup
Olive oil (liquid)	1 liter	33.8 Fl oz
Eggs	1 egg	1 egg
Rice	1 cup (200g)	6.5 oz
Pasta (dry)	100 grams	3.5 ounces
Ground meat (beef, lamb, etc.)	100 grams	3.5 ounces
Fresh herbs (parsley, basil)	1 bunch	1 bunch
Fresh vegetables (tomatoes, cucumbers)	1 medium	1 medium
Wine (bottle)	750 milliliters	25.4 Fl oz

These conversions will help ensure that your Mediterranean recipes turn out just right, no matter what unit of measurement you're using.

Index of Mediterranean Ingredients and Recipes

A

- **Assyrtiko** (Greece) - A crisp white wine variety perfect with seafood.
- **Avocado** - Often used in Mediterranean salads and spreads.

B

- **Baba Ghanoush** - A smoky eggplant dip from the Levant.
- **Baklava** - A sweet pastry made of thin layers of dough, nuts, and honey syrup.

C

- **Chickpeas** - A staple legume used in hummus, salads, and stews.
- **Couscous** - A small, steamed wheat pasta often served with stews.

D

- **Dolma** - Stuffed grape leaves, typically filled with rice and herbs.
- **Dukkha** - A spice mix used for dipping bread, often with olive oil.

E

- **Eggplant** - A key vegetable in Mediterranean dishes like moussaka and baba ghanoush.

THE MEDITERRANEAN LIFESTYLE

F

- **Feta** - A brined cheese from Greece, often crumbled over salads or baked into pies.

G

- **Gnocchi** - A type of pasta made from potatoes, commonly served with sauces in Italy.

Glossary of Mediterranean Cooking Terms

Al Dente – An Italian term meaning "to the tooth." It refers to cooking pasta or vegetables until they are firm to the bite, not overcooked or soft.

Braise – A slow-cooking method where meat or vegetables are first browned in oil and then simmered in a small amount of liquid for a long time.

Couscous – A North African dish made from steamed semolina grains. It's often served as a side dish or base for stews.

Frittata – An Italian-style omelet that is often filled with vegetables, cheese, and herbs.

Garnish – A small, decorative addition to a dish meant to enhance its appearance and flavor, such as fresh herbs or a drizzle of olive oil.

Meze – A selection of small dishes served as appetizers in Mediterranean cuisines, particularly in the Middle East and the Balkans.

Olives – Both the fruit and oil are fundamental to Mediterranean cooking, used in salads, tapenade, and as a base for many sauces.

Sauté – To cook food quickly in a small amount of oil or butter over high heat.

Tagine – A traditional Moroccan stew that is slow-cooked in a special clay pot with a conical lid, often made with lamb, chicken, or vegetables.

Tzatziki – A yogurt-based sauce or dip from Greece, typically made with cucumber, garlic, and herbs like dill or mint.

Za'atar – A Middle Eastern spice blend made from thyme, sesame seeds, sumac, and other spices, commonly used in breads, meats, and salads.

THE MEDITERRANEAN LIFESTYLE

Conclusion

As we come to the end of this culinary journey through the Mediterranean, I hope you feel inspired, empowered, and excited to embrace a way of eating and living that is as nourishing for the soul as it is for the body. The Mediterranean diet is not just a collection of recipes, but a celebration of **fresh, vibrant ingredients**, **seasonal eating**, and the joy of sharing meals with loved ones. By incorporating the flavors and principles of the Mediterranean into your daily life, you can not only improve your health but also enrich your relationships and overall well-being.

Whether you're savoring a bowl of **Greek yogurt** with honey, enjoying a hearty **Moroccan tagine**, or indulging in a classic **Italian pasta**, the Mediterranean diet invites you to slow down, appreciate the beauty of fresh food, and reconnect with the simple pleasures of life. From the benefits of **heart health** to **mental clarity**, the Mediterranean way of eating offers a path to a longer, healthier life—without compromising on taste or enjoyment.

Remember, the beauty of Mediterranean cuisine lies in its **flexibility**—feel free to adjust recipes to suit your tastes, preferences, and dietary needs. This book is just the beginning of your journey. As you continue to explore, experiment, and adapt, you'll find that the Mediterranean way of eating is not only sustainable but also endlessly satisfying.

May your journey through the world of Mediterranean flavors be filled with joy, health, and the simple pleasures of life. Bon appétit!

Printed in Great Britain
by Amazon